# Back To Basics

Parenting Principles:
A Biblical
Perspective

## By Daniel Taddeo

Fairway Press
Lima, Ohio

# BACK TO BASICS

FIRST EDITION
Copyright © 1993 by
Daniel Taddeo

I want to express my appreciation to all who have shared their light in my life, much of which is reflected in the following pages. A special thanks to Nancy Kilhenny for her help in preparing the manuscript.

7970 / ISBN 1-55673-546-4

*Dedicated to my children:*
*Laurie Ann, Dana Lynn, Christian Daniel*

*"You have exalted above all things your name and your word."*

— *Psalm 138.2*

# Table Of Contents

# Preface

The birth of a child is a miracle. A gift from God created in His image. Nothing has greater value in His eyes. People have children for different reasons. It is very important parents understand their reasons because they have a tremendous impact on the parent/child relationship. God expects parents to faithfully nurture their children.

Parenting is the greatest challenge most adults will ever face. I once heard a mother remark that her former pressure-filled full-time job was a cakewalk in comparison to full-time parenthood. Isn't that the truth! In addition to the long hours of physical care for children, being responsible for their moral, spiritual and emotional needs is an awesome task. However, it can also be one of life's most rewarding experiences when good parenting principles are practiced. What follows is intended to help make this possible.

*Back To Basics* identifies 61 different areas important to parenting. The reader is told what the topic is, why it's important to parents and children and suggestions on how to put the applied principles into practice. Selected Bible passages accompany each topic and serve as the authority. Though not exhaustive, they're ones I believe parents need to address for successful parenting. They aren't speculative. They're grounded in Scripture. And they have withstood the test of time.

The purpose of this book is not to list preset, hard-and-fast rules and solutions for raising children. But rather to sensitize parents to the important issues of child-rearing. *Back To Basics* serves as a road map to parenting: guidelines that benefit children as well as parents.

As a counselor, I was constantly searching for answers to such questions as to why certain children felt accepted while others felt rejected? Why certain ones had high self-esteem while others felt unworthy? Why certain children felt loved while others didn't? Why certain ones succeeded while others failed? The conclusion that I came to was that children reared by parents who lived by the Ten Commandments was the single most important factor that accounted for the differences in their behavior.

From that time on I sensed a calling to share that knowledge. I believe God has a plan for each and every child. He holds parents accountable for helping that child discover what that plan is. Parents must guard against making their children into what they think they ought to be rather than what God created them to be. This becomes possible when parents follow time-tested parenting principles grounded in the Bible.

*Back To Basics* speaks to parents about the impact home environment has on children during the pre-school years. If children don't learn certain things during these critical years, they may not learn them at all because the season will have passed them by. Remember, much of what is displayed in adults was learned in childhood before children walk, talk or attend school. The adult example remains the most dominant force in child development.

The family is the very foundation upon which society rests. It's the first and often the only place where children learn the right values to see them through adulthood, a place where they can be nurtured, loved and accepted as God intended.

The selected Bible passages quoted serve as the inspiration for *Back To Basics*. They are taken from *The New King James Version*. It is my hope and prayer that these principles will equip the reader with time-tested guidelines so necessary in the restoration and preservation of the family as ordained by God. May they honor and glorify His name.

# Accountability

Children need to understand that God holds them responsible for what they are, for what they have been given, and for what they do with their gifts. That's accountability. "So then each of us shall give account of himself to God."[1] " 'But I say to you that for every idle (careless) word men may speak, they will give account of it in the day of judgment.' "[2] Children do have to try to look and be like everybody else, nor be something or someone they are not. God holds them accountable for what they are. No more, no less. "They will give an account to Him who is ready to judge the living and the dead."[3] The Prophet Daniel put it this way: ". . . The court was seated, and the books (which contain a complete record of everybody's life on earth) were opened."[4]

Children will learn about accountability from you. This important task is not to be left to others. Children learn right from wrong early in life, but at times they may choose to do wrong anyway. Many think they can do what they want as long as nobody finds out. It should be made very clear to them that God knows their every word, thought and deed before they do! ". . . For there is nothing covered that will not be revealed, and hidden that will not be unknown."[5]

---

1. Rom. 14.12; 2. Matt. 12.36; 3. 1 Pet 4.5; 4. Dan. 7.10; 5. Matt. 10.26.

# Anger

Anger is good for you provided it's the right kind. The Bible talks about two kinds of anger: sinful and righteous. Sinful anger is excessive, uncontrolled rage whose intent is to punish and injure and that's not good. But righteous anger is controlled, thereby able to accomplish good. " 'Be angry and do not sin . . .' "[1] You can use anger with positive results. "Let no corrupt word proceed out of your mouth, but what is good for necessary edification (instruction) that it may impart grace to the hearers."[2]

Hidden or denied anger may cause serious emotional and physical problems. Unresolved anger may surface in the form of headaches, stomach pains, ulcers, nail-biting, lying, cheating, rebellious school behavior, and high absenteeism, to mention a few. The sooner anger is confronted, the sooner it can be defused. ". . . Do not let the sun go down on your wrath . . . ."[3] Don't allow it to fester. ". . . Let every man be swift to hear, slow to speak, slow to wrath; for the wrath of man does not produce the righteousness of God."[4] Identifying the source of anger helps children avoid over-reacting.

Children learn how to handle anger by observing their parents. God expresses his wisdom in the following passage: "He who is slow to wrath has great understanding, but he who is impulsive exalts folly."[5] "A soft answer turns away wrath, but a harsh word stirs up anger."[6] "In the multitude of words sin is not lacking, but he who restrains his lips is wise."[7] "Let all bitterness, wrath, anger, clamor (yelling), and evil speaking be put away from you with all malice (deliberate intent)."[8] "Do not be rash (reckless) with your mouth, and let not your heart utter anything hastily before God."[9] When children get

10

angry, parents should first help them recognize it; second, admit it; and third, take responsible action in dealing with it. The best cure for anger is to do an unexpected kindness for the person he or she is angry at. This behavior will say "I am sorry" better than any words.

---

1. Eph. 4.26; 2. Eph. 4.29; 3. Eph. 4.26; 4. James 1.19, 20; 5. Prov. 14:29; 6. Prov. 15.1; 7. Prov. 10.19; 8. Eph. 4.31; Eccles. 5.2.

# Attitude

Attitude dictates our behavior. That's why it's so important to have a good one. "For as he thinks in his heart, so is he ...."[1] No matter what the facts or circumstances, we have the choice and power to choose the attitude we take toward those facts and circumstances.

With children, attitude can be even more important than facts. Why? Because it depends on how they perceive the facts. Children with similar makeup and circumstances often see themselves differently. For example: some feel accepted while others feel rejected; some have high self-esteem while others feel unworthy; some feel appreciated while others do not; some see God as condemning while others see Him as loving, caring and forgiving. Why?

Parents need to be aware of how their attitudes affect their children. Children tend to adopt their parents' attitudes quite early in life. For example, when parents focus on the negative, children tend to do the same. But when parents look for the positive, children will learn that it is what is expected of them. The environment in which children are reared has so much to do with their attitudes about life.

The Bible tells us to take a positive attitude toward everyone and everything. To fill our thoughts and conversations with the good and the uplifting. "... Whatever things are true, whatever things are noble, whatever things are just, whatever things are pure, whatever things are lovely, whatever things are of good report, if there is any virtue and if there is anything praiseworthy — meditate on these things."[2] Focusing on positive attitudes prevents and forces out negative ones. Parents and children alike are what they think.

12

Parents need to encourage their children to focus on the positive aspects of life. Think good thoughts. Look for the best in others. Always treat others the way they want to be treated. Help them to strive to make others feel better. In so doing, they will feel better about themselves. They need to learn that the full life is experienced in direct proportion to how they give of themselves.

The Bible says, "Let this mind be in you which was also in Christ Jesus ..."[3] That God is an unchanging light. Children can move closer to the light and see their way better; or they can move away from it and struggle in the darkness. When their attitude is in line with God's word, everything they do will turn out right. Those who follow Jesus reflect His glory no matter what their path or station in life. "I can do all things through Christ who strengthens me."[4] Parents need to remind their children that they, and not circumstances, are responsible for their attitude.

Children's attitudes dictate their actions. If their attitudes are God-centered, they are likely to act positively and responsibly. If they are self-centered, they are likely to act negatively and selfishly.

---

1. Prov. 23.7; 2. Phil. 4.8; 3. Phil. 2.5; 4. Phil. 4.13.

# Blame

The blame game is as old as the Garden of Eden. Can't you just see Adam and Eve pointing fingers at each other and at that grinning serpent? God gave man the freedom to choose. When God confronted him, Adam blamed Eve and Eve blamed the devil and neither accepted the responsibility for disobeying God. Not much has changed. We blame friends, parents, home, environment, circumstances — anyone but ourselves.

It's a hard lesson but children must be taught to accept responsibility for their actions rather than blame others. They have to understand that if they commit wrong acts they will suffer the consequences. When they don't accept blame their destructive behavior can go unchecked and things can go from bad to worse. If you allow kids to place blame, you're setting in motion a vicious circle of behavior.

People who blame are basically insecure, have low self-esteem and do not really like themselves. This may be the result when children have been excessively criticized and resort to blaming as a means of defending themselves. It is very important that parents avoid disciplining their children in front of others whenever possible. Little good and much harm comes from embarrassing, humiliating and stripping children of their dignity. "Fathers (and mothers) do not provoke your children, lest they become discouraged."[1]

It is very easy to fall into the trap of making excuses to rationalize behavior. Resist the temptation to blame and thereby set a good example for your children. Teach them to accept responsibility for their actions and not resort to making excuses and blaming others. It's a grave injustice to overlook irresponsible behavior in children and bail them out rather than letting them face the consequences of their actions.

---

1. Col. 3.21

# Character

Isn't building character simply teaching right from wrong? Well, yes, but it isn't always that simple. Good character takes a long time to shape and there are plenty of passages in the Bible to support its value. God's plan and purpose is to develop righteous character in each of us: qualities such as humility, tolerance, honesty, trustworthiness and dependability.

Nothing we could think, say or do comes even close to being as important as good character. The number one concern in life is to develop the character required for eternity. It is the only thing we take with us when we cross over from this life to life eternal. After death, character is the only thing that counts. Good character is what we look for in others. It is what employers look for in us and most importantly, this is what God looks for in us. How we accomplish something should always have priority over what we accomplish.

Character development is the primary responsibility of parents. If good character traits are not instilled in children early, often they are not learned at all. Too often we place more emphasis on what children achieve rather than how they learn and interact with others. Scripture cautions us that good character development will not be easy and requires that children be closely supervised. "Do not be deceived: evil company corrupts good habits."[1]

Difficulty is an essential ingredient for character development and spiritual growth. Therefore, children will require praise and encouragement. ". . . But we also glory in tribulations (sufferings), knowing that tribulation produces perseverance; And perseverance, character; and character, hope. Now hope does not disappoint . . . ."[2] Hope is one of God's greatest blessings. Children need to be reminded that during time of deep trials and tribulation, God is their refuge where they can find comfort in the assurance that pain and suffering serve a purpose even though they may not understand it at the time. The Godly character parents help their children build will serve them well in this life and the next.

---

1. 1 Cor. 15.33; 2. Rom. 5.3-5.

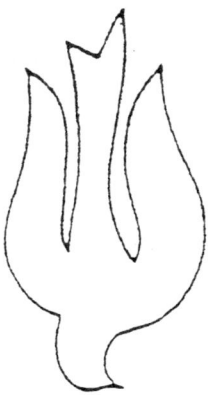

# Contentment

Contentment is experienced only when we place Godly limits on our requirements, desires and actions. Then we can feel satisfied with our possessions, status and circumstances. Contentment says, I am satisfied with what I have at this moment regardless of what my hopes may be for the future. "... Be content with such things as you have ...."[1] This is perfect contentment and is what God intends for each of His children. "Now godliness with contentment is great gain."[2] Knowing and accepting limts leads to contentment and it's an important lesson to instill in children. Typically, kids think that when they get more, then they will be satisfied. We all know that the next need is over the horizon. The world is filled with disappointed people seeking contentment from material possessions. Contentment is rooted in what people are, not on what they have.

Children need to be taught how to channel their discontentment. The key to contentment is not looking inward but rather looking upward. " '... Not My will but yours be done.' "[3], in all situations in life. The Apostle Paul's secret for living out God's will in his life was his intimate relationship with Christ. In spite of his many trials, he managed to live a very contented life as noted in the following passage: "... For I have learned in whatever state I am, to be content: I know how to be abased (humble) and I know to abound. Everywhere and in all things I have learned both to be full and to be hungry, both to abound and to suffer need. I can do all things through Christ who strengthens me."[4]

When children realize the value in God's love, they will discover His peace and joy. No matter what circumstances surround them, if they live each day to glorify Him, then each day will be a perfect day. As difficult as this is to understand, it is very comforting for children to know, " '... With God all things are possible ...' "[5]

1. Heb. 13.5; 2. 1 Tim. 6.6; 3. Luke 22.42; 4. Phil. 4.11-13; 5. Matt. 19.26.

# Death

Let's be honest: death isn't a popular topic for discussion with children. When a loved one dies it seems unpleasant, depressing. But it doesn't have to be that way. What a perfect opportunity to share the Easter story. Jesus tells us, " 'Most assuredly, I say to you, he who hears My words and believes in Him who sent Me has everlasting life, and shall not come into judgment, but has passed from death to life.' "[1] Remember to be honest. Talk about death openly, including funeral arrangements. Answer the question all children ask: "What happens to people when they die?" The way death is viewed makes a big difference in how people live their lives. " '. . . I am the resurrection and the life. He who believes in Me, though he may die, he shall live.' "[2] God provides the hope children need to face the fear, sorrow and pain of death. It is very sad to lose loved ones for the believer, death is like falling asleep. When they awake they will be in the presence of the Lord. " . . . To be absent from the body and to be present with the Lord."[3] It is birth into a new world. Death has to occur first before the new life can begin.

Children need a lot of help and support facing things they can't fully understand like death. Departed loved ones leave a great void in their lives that needs to be filled. The Twenty-Third Psalm can provide much comfort to adults as well as children during such times.

> *The Lord is my shepherd; I shall not want.*
> *He makes me to lie down in green pastures; He leads me beside the still waters.*
> *He restores my soul; He leads me in the paths of righteousness for His name's sake.*

*Yeah, though I walk through the valley of the shadow of death, I will fear no evil; for You are with me; Your rod and Your staff, they comfort me.*

*You prepare a table before me in the presence of my enemies; You anoint my head with oil; My cup runs over.*

*Surely goodness and mercy shall follow me all the days of my life; and I will dwell in the house of the Lord forever.*

Children need to know that grieving the loss of loved ones is not only appropriate, it's encouraged. At the same time they need reminding to take comfort in the knowledge that their loved ones are in God's presence and that they can look forward to being united with them in the life after in eternity.

---

1. John 5.24; 2. John 11.25; 3. 2 Cor. 5.8.

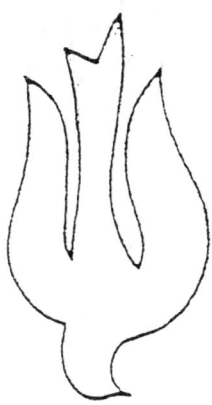

# Discipline

When was the last time you heard yourself saying, "This hurts me more than it's going to hurt you?" Disciplining children is painful and unpleasant but remember it's truly an expression of love. Of course, children being corrected don't readily thank you for loving them so much but it is often necessary.

Our Heavenly Father says, " 'As many as I love, I rebuke and chasten.' "[1] He is setting limits on us and that's what we need to do with our kids. There is mutual love and respect between parents and children when discipline is executed in a fair, firm and friendly manner. You and your spouse should be united in all aspects of child rearing, otherwise children are quick to take advantage when mothers and fathers fail to speak as one voice.

There is a right time to discipline and you have to make that decision, but make it early. Children are much more receptive early in life because they basically want to please and be accepted and there is little or no outside influence. "Do not withhold correction from a child . . ."[2] If you count on school to teach discipline, you are in for a big disappointment. When seeds are not planted at the right time, they either do poorly or do not grow at all no matter what we do.

Parents should always try to discipline from a positive point of view by rewarding good behavior. Lead children rather than order them. Avoid undesirable situations and circumstances when possible. Catch them doing something right and tell them about it. Try to resolve conflicts by talking it over at their level. However, too much talk can make matters worse because of the limited reasoning ability of children.

Another means of disciplining young children is spanking. Some parents do not use it. Others abuse it. Spanking, as a means of communicating with children, is not a license for beating children. The Bible says, "The rod and rebuke give wisdom, but a child left to himself brings shame to his mother. Correct your son, and he will give you rest; yes, he will give delight to your soul."[3] "He who spares his rod hates his son, but he who loves him disciplines him promptly."[4] "Train up a child in the way he should go and when he is old he will not depart from it."[5] Physical punishment along with other means of disciplining is most effective when reasoning is very limited such as during the pre-school years.

All other means of disciplining should be exhausted before resorting to spanking because children respond differently. To spank children when they do not understand why they are being spanked is cruel and inexcusable. If spanking is used, it should be only a single open hand on children's bottoms. Parents should not assume spanking will always produce favorable results. But the risks of spanking will always be less than the danger of not correcting the matter. As acceptable behavior patterns are established and understanding increases, physical punishment as a means of disciplining should cease.

Solomon, the author of proverbs, urges parents to learn the unique traits of their children. He knew that discipline, to be effective, must be adapted to children so they will respond to it. And as they mature be shaped by it. "Foolishness is bound up in the heart of a child; the root of correction will drive it far from him."[6]

Parents should not feel they are doing something wrong or feel guilty when they say "no" to their children. In many instances this is exactly what they need. It is important parents help their children recognize the difference between their wants and their needs and then respond accordingly. Because parents are so much more knowledgeable about what is right and proper, children should adjust to parents and not the other way around. Disciplined children are happy children. The un-disciplined children are not.

_____

1. Rev. 3.19; 2. Prov. 23.13; 3. Prov. 29.15, 17; 4. Prov. 13.24; 5. Prov. 22.6; 6. Prov. 22.15.

# Education

There is much concern about education in America. One such area of concern is the declining trend in educational standards and the drop in standardized achievement test scores. Many of the reasons focus on dangers in the family: two working parents, more single-parent families, less parental involvement in children's education, student mental health problems, growing student disobedience, unexcused absences and tardiness, vandalism, theft, lying, cheating, drugs, alcohol and teenage pregnancies. Many more reasons could be added to this list. Parents tend to blame the schools when the students do not do well. This is unfortunate because most of the time, the school is simply a reflection of the homes students come from.

Parents must accept the fact that it is they, and not the school who are ultimately responsible for their children's education. Many of their teachers will be very ordinary men and women. A few will be exceptionally outstanding and a few will actually do more harm than good to the students they teach. During the first one hundred fifty years of compulsory public education, moral and spiritual values had an important role in the public school. Recent court rulings have changed all that. Many public schools pride themselves in providing value-free education to their students. This, of course, is impossible. They have merely substituted other values in their place.

The pre-school years are the most critical in a child's development. Those years form the foundation of future performance. The values you instill in your children is a major factor of how they will do in school. Children become better at what they bring to school. For example, if they learn to respect authority at home, they will respect the teacher and benefit from what school has to offer. If they come as liars and cheaters, they will become better liars and cheaters. The same applies to many of the other character traits children bring to school.

So what should you expect your child to learn in school? There are many things beyond sheer academics and the values discussed above. They should learn:

1. How to learn. This will equip children with the ability to handle all the things that may confront them later in life that they did not learn at home or at school;

2. Where to find out information to solve problems;

3. How to think;

4. How to better express one's self;

5. The importance of completing work on time;

6. How to follow directions;

7. Learn to exercise self-discipline;

8. Reason should rule over emotion. Do what needs to be done — like it or not;

9. Learn new concepts, attitudes and values that are acceptable to God.

You can do more to reverse the downward trend in standardized achievement test scores than any other single element in our society. When you supervise education at home and in school, you equip your kids with the knowledge, skills, attitudes and all the other moral and spiritual characteristics so necessary for successful personal and family living.

# Example

The power of the example has no limits. Nowhere is this more true than in parenting. The following actions by parents will do much to instill these same qualities in their children.

1. Count blessings rather than troubles
2. Praise rather than criticize
3. Be positive rather than negative
4. Give rather than receive
5. Judge self rather than others
6. Be quick to listen and slow to anger
7. Seek spiritual rather than worldly values
8. Be humble rather than proud
9. Prize good character rather than personal gain
10. Be judged rather than judge
11. Serve rather than be served
12. Be honest rather than dishonest
13. Forgive rather than resent
14. Be merciful rather than insulting
15. Pray for our enemies rather than hate them
16. Be patient rather than intolerant
17. Build others up rather than tear them down
18. Be last rather than first
19. Give praise rather than seek it
20. Be God-centered rather than self-centered

Parents soon discover it's not easy following Biblical principles during the parenting years. But, God's power will sustain them because they are doing His will. "For whatever a man sows, that he will also reap .... And let us not grow weary while doing good, for in due season we shall reap if we do not lose heart."[1] Though these actions are not natural to the human heart, they can accomplish amazing things when practiced in the power of the spirit.

Parents will not be judged simply by how well they kept God's commandments, but how well they have allowed the love of Christ to live through them.

---

1. Gal. 6.7, 8.

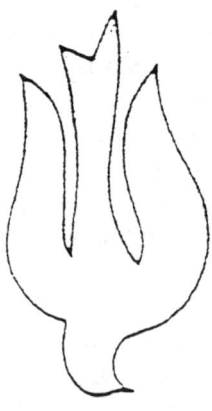

# Expectations

What do you expect of your children? Think long and hard so that you don't put undue pressure on them. Unrealistic expectations can be a source of much irritation and disappointment for both parents and children. The wider the gap between what parents think and the actual facts, the greater the unhappiness. When children get the message that nothing they do is quite good enough, they soon view themselves as failures and conduct themselves accordingly.

It is important that parents have reasonable, realistic and fair expectations for their children. When they do not, children live in fear of the consequences of disappointing their parents. This ought not be. "For God has not given us a spirit of fear, but of power and of love and of a sound mind."[1] When children cannot please their parents, they often resort to making excuses in order to survive. Making excuses in one area may carry over to other areas and be adopted as a way of coping in the family.

It becomes easier and easier to make excuses rather than try to meet even the attainable expectations. This teaches children to be dishonest. If they cannot be honest with their parents and themselves, they surely will not be honest with others. Children who become good at making excuses seldom become good at anything else. Basically, children really do want to please their parents.

When parental expectations are self-directed rather than God-directed, disappointment, frustration and unhappiness are sure to follow for both parents and children. "In all your ways acknowledge Him, and He shall direct your paths."[2] God has provided His complete infallible Word as a guide for parenting. God is to parents what parents are to children. Once they know what God expects of them, their expectations for their children will be appropriate.

God's word says, "... It is required in stewards that one be found faithful."[3] This means making the best use of our talents. "Having then gifts differing according to the grace that is given to us, let us use them ..."[4] It is cruel to expect behavior from children they are incapable of giving. There is nothing wrong with parents having high expectations for their children, but they must be ready and willing to settle for the children's best. God holds them accountable for doing only their best with the gifts they have been given.

---

1. 2 Tim. 1.7; 2. Prov. 3.6; 3. 1 Cor. 4.2; 4. Rom. 12.6.

# Faith

Faith is total trust in God, believing everything about Him as recorded in the Bible. "Now faith is the substance of things hoped for, the evidence of things not seen."[1] "That your faith should not be in the wisdom of men but in the power of God."[2] Those with strong faith do not let circumstances cause them to doubt God.

It is important for children to sense this faith in their parents so they will believe that God will do what He promises. Faith overcomes fear, doubt and depression and replaces them with peace, joy and confidence. It also helps children turn from wrong to right. " '... According to your faith let it be to you ...' "[3] Faith gives children access to God. It equips them with His power to cope with whatever may confront them in life. The greater their faith, the greater the presence of God in their lives. And when they are right with God, they are right with the world.

Children need to be taught that they must come to God in faith. Faith is the link between God and them. Their approach to faith is one of submission to God and His will. Faith concedes that God is in control. "So then faith comes by hearing, and hearing by the word of God."[4] Faith comes through prayer, attending church and serving others. "... Faith by itself, if it does not have works, is dead."[5]

All who come to God must come the same way — in child-like faith. How important we are? How much money we have? How much education we have? How smart we are? None of these will impress God. What's more, they can even be a hindrance. In reality, little children claim none of these

31

things. Yet God tells us to approach Him with the mind set of children: helpless, dependent, trusting, thankful, humble, in awe and blind faith.

---

1. Heb. 11.1; 2. 1 Cor. 2.5; 3. Matt. 9.29; 4. Rom. 10.17; 5. James 2.17.

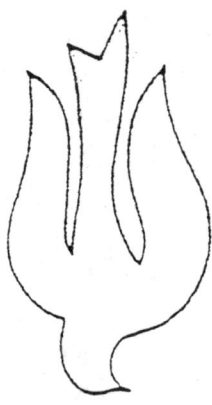

# Family

The family is the institution in any society that protects and dignifies the individual. It is where individual rights and responsibilities should be nurtured, transmitted and defended.

The family is our foundation. It is the first and often the only place where children learn principles and values that take them through adulthood; a place where they can be nurtured, loved and accepted for what they are.

The love of God binds families together like nothing else. But when families drift away from Biblical principles scriptures tell us, "Unless the Lord builds the house, they labor in vain who builds it . . . ."[1] The consequences of not abiding in God's word include: disrespect for law and order and moral deterioration of the family. Similar conditions prompted Joshua, the Israelite leader, to say, " '. . . Choose for yourselves this day whom you will serve . . . But as for me and my house, we will serve the Lord.' "[2] In the New Testament are recorded the words, " '. . . Believe in the Lord Jesus Christ and you will be saved, you and your household . . .' "[3] When Biblical principles are practiced in the home, children sense that family comes first.

Children thrive when parents provide strong leadership in the family. Building family ties and loyalty can be achieved through activities such as family devotions, church attendance, Bible study, pleasant meal time conditions, family picnics, vacations, family reunions, keeping family traditions alive and starting new traditions. These experiences all contribute to enrich and strengthen the family. Entire civilizations rise and fall on the strength of the family. A Chinese Proverb states:

*"If there is righteousness in the heart,*
*There will be beauty (grace) in the character.*
*If there be beauty in the character,*
*There is harmony in the home.*
*If there is harmony in the home,*
*There will be order in the nation.*
*When there is order in the nation,*
*There will be peace in the world."*

---

1. Ps. 127.1; 2. Josh. 24.15; 3. Acts 16.31.

# Fear

What's the difference between good fear and bad fear? Bad fear is worldly, fear of life-threatening consequences. It can be so terrifying that it can make you helpless and powerless to act. Good fear is just the opposite. It's Godly. Fear of the Lord is reverent awe for the holiness of God. "The fear of the Lord is the beginning of wisdom; a good understanding have all those who do His commandments ...."[1] "Do not be wise in your own eyes; fear the Lord and depart from evil."[2] "The fear of the Lord is a fountain of life ...."[3] Godly fear is one of the greatest motivators in life.

Children need to understand that living with worldly fears such as failure, rejection, loneliness, doubt and death, our greatest fear, is a fact of life. But God will help them through all their worldly fears. When children approach the unknown they will experience a certain amount of fear. Parents can help them through these times by reminding them of the many comforting Biblical passages such as: " '... The Lord is my helper; I will not fear. What can man do to me?' "[4] " '... Be strong and be of good courage; do not be afraid nor be dismayed, for the Lord your God is with you wherever you go.' "[5] "The Lord is my light and my salvation; whom shall I fear? The Lord is the strength of my life; of whom shall I be afraid?"[6]

Children can learn to control their fears by learning to trust God in everything. The more they fill their minds with God the less room for fears to find a home. "There is no fear in love; but perfect love casts out fear, because fear involves torment. But he who fears has not been made perfect in love."[7] Children need to be reminded that the more they love and trust God the less intense their fears. Also, God's love allows them to see others as God sees them — as one of his own. Jesus says, " 'Be of good cheer! It is I; do not be afraid.' "[8] Children need to be encouraged to ask God for strength to deal with all the fear that will surface. God sent Christ into the world to remove their fears, doubts and loneliness. Trusting Him is the only way to free themselves from the bondage of fear.

---

1. Ps. 111.10; 2. Prov. 3.7; 3. Prov. 14.27; 4. Heb. 13.6; 5. Josh 1.9; 6. Ps. 27.1; 7. 1 John 4.18; 8. Matt. 14.27.

# Forgiveness

Forgiveness means to pardon; a matter of letting go of resentment, anger and deep-seated hatred of others and at times ourselves. Forgiveness frees and heals the forgiver and eventually the forgiven. Our greatest need after salvation is forgiveness. Children need to know that Jesus and parents love them and forgive them when they sin. It's also important for you to teach your children how to forgive others.

Not forgiving is harmful. The medical profession is convinced that emotions such as anger, hatred, resentment, envy and fear are at the root of most physical ailments. Not forgiving means being imprisoned by the past. Forgiveness frees us from that past.

Use these passages to illustrate forgiveness to your children: "If we confess our sins, He is faithful and just to forgive us our sins and to cleanse us from all unrighteousness."[1] "As far as the east is from the west, so far has HE removed our transgressions from us."[2] Even while Jesus suffered on the cross HE said, " 'Father, forgive them, for they do not know what they do ...' "[3]

Because God freely forgives us, we are asked to forgive others when they wrong us. " '... If you have anything against anyone, forgive him, that your Father in heaven may also forgive you your trespasses.' "[4] And be kind to one another, tenderhearted, forgiving one another, even as God in Christ forgave you."[5] " 'Judge not, and you shall not be judged. Condemn not, and you shall not be condemned. Forgive, and you will be forgiven.' "[6] It is in giving that we receive.

Forgiveness is a recurring theme in the Bible. When we pray the Lord's Prayer, "Forgive us our debts (sins) as we forgive our debtors.'"[7] We ask God to forgive us according to our forgiveness of others. The forgiveness we give determines the forgiveness we receive.

---

1. 1 John 1.9; 2. Ps. 103.12; 3. Luke 23.34; 4. Mark 11.25; 5. Eph. 4.32; 6. Luke 6.37; 7. Matt. 6.12.

# Freedom

Freedom is something we all want. It is, however, a gift from God to believers. Until we realize this true freedom will continue to escape us. As soon as we acknowledge that God is the source of freedom we can begin to live our lives as God would have us live; love as God would have us love, and give as God would have us give. Freedom to live, love and give become inseparable.

Many people believe that if we could do whatever we wanted, whenever we wanted, only then could we be free. The exact opposite is true. Try to imagine the quality of life if people did everything they thought was right rather than submitting to any laws. The advantage of living begins with submission. "Submit to God. Resist the devil and he will flee from you."[1] We have the most freedom when we live according to God's word. " 'And you shall know the truth and the truth shall make you free.' "[2]

Children need to know that when God created man in HIS own image he was perfect and then He gave man the freedom of choice. "And the Lord God commanded the man, saying, 'Of every tree of knowledge of good and evil you shall not eat, ... for in the day that you eat of it you shall surely die.' "[3] Man disobeyed. Because of this children too must choose between good and evil. God does not force one or the other upon anyone. "Do you not know to whom you present yourselves slaves to obey, you are that one's slave whom you obey, whether of sin leading to death, or of obedience leading to righteousness .... And having been set free from sin, you became slaves of righteousness."[4]

39

Children will live according to the master they choose — sin or God but they need your help to make the right choice. Sin will hold them in bondage. Christ liberates them from that bondage. They are helpless to free themselves and must rely on a higher power. " 'Therefore if the SON makes you free, you shall be free indeed.' "[5]

Trust and faith in Christ is the key that releases children from the prison of sin and sets them free. They can claim this freedom when they:

1. accept Jesus as their personal Savior
2. confess their faith in HIM
3. trust their lives to HIM
4. submit their will to HIS
5. withhold nothing from HIM
6. believe true freedom comes only through HIM
7. study HIS word

A train is free to travel only if it stays on the railroad tracks. God's laws allow children to be all they can possibly be without hurting themselves and serve others as well. It is in serving Christ they will find true freedom, joy and peace . . . "Where the Spirit of the Lord is, there is liberty (freedom)."[6]

---

1. James 4.7; 2. John 8.32; 3. Gen. 2.16, 17; 4. Rom. 6.16, 18; 5. John 8.36; 6. 2 Cor. 3.17.

# Friends

Friends are special people we admire and hold in high esteem. They help us to live better lives, and we all need them. Children are no exception. Adults and children alike can get so desperate for friendship they even try to buy it in an effort to avoid rejection. Parents need to teach their children that in order to have friends they must be one themselves. Children need to ask themselves how they would want their friends to think of them. Then get on with doing it. Here's some specific actions they can take:

1. Loving — " 'A new commandment I give to you, that you love one another; as I have loved you, that you also love one another.' "[1] " 'Greater love has no one than this, than to lay down one's life for his friends.' "[2]
2. Friendliness — "A man who has friends must himself be friendly ...."[3]
3. Persistence — "A friend loves at all times."[4]
4. Loyalty — "Do not forsake your own friend ...."[5]
5. Peacemaking — "... Let us pursue the things which make for peace and the things by which one may edify another."[6]
6. Listening — "Let every man be swift to hear, slow to speak, slow to wrath."[7]
7. Praising and Encouraging — "Rejoice with those who rejoice, and weep with those who weep."[8]
8. Sincerity — "Let each of you look out not only for his own interests, but also for the interests of others."[9]
9. Supporting — "As iron sharpens iron, so a man sharpens the countenance (approval) of his friends."[10]

The list of qualities for being a friend is endless. Children should be taught that friendship just doesn't happen. Seeds have to be planted and cultivated. They have to work at it. Friendship is built more on giving and less on taking. Emphasis should always be more on being a friend rather than finding one. Children have to like themselves before they can like others and have others like them. Children who show their enthusiasm for life and encourage others with sincere love, praise, genuine concern and acceptance of others will never lack friends.

Everyone needs at least one good friend. Fortunately, everyone is guaranteed one. That person is Jesus. It is reassuring to know that if their earthly friends let them down, children will still always have Jesus as their friend. He will never let them down. He knows all about them and loves them just as they are. He understands everything about them and promises to be their friend forever. In the words of the familiar hymn:

> *"What a Friend we have in Jesus, all our sins and griefs to bear! What a privilege to carry, everything to God in prayer! Oh, what peace we often forfeit, Oh, what needless pain we bear, All, because we do not carry, everything to God in prayer! ...*

Can we find a Friend so faithful who will all our sorrows share? Jesus knows our every weakness, "take it to the Lord in prayer."

---

1. John 13.34; 2. John 15.13; 3. Prov. 18.24; 4. Prov. 17.17; 5. Prov. 27.10; 6. Rom. 14.19; 7. James 1.19; 8. Rom. 12.15; 9. Phil. 2.4; 10. Prov. 27.17.

# Fruit Of The Spirit

Scripture teaches that if we "walk in the Spirit" we will be recipients of its fruit.[1] The fruit of the Spirit includes:

1. LOVE — loving others the way God loves us.
2. JOY — being happy about all God represents.
3. PEACE — an undisturbed state of mind because God is in control.
4. LONG SUFFERING (patience) — overcoming our trials rather than have them overcome us.
4. KINDNESS — wanting the best for others.
6. GOODNESS — doing what is right.
7. FAITHFULNESS — unquestioning belief, trust and reliance on God.
8. GENTLENESS — being considerate of other people's shortcomings.
9. SELF-CONTROL — resisting temptations that are unacceptable to God.

At some point in their development children are going to ask questions like: "Why was I born?" "What is the purpose of life?" Parents need to know the answers to questions like these. There is great purpose in human life. " ... Let us make man in our image," God said.[2] This means, then, with God's help, people can acquire the kind of character God has. God made people like HIMSELF. So, anyone who obeys God's commandments and expresses HIS love by thought, word and action is becoming like God.

Children should be told that the main reason they were born is to represent God by bearing HIS Fruit. Jesus said, "I am the true vine, and my Father is the vinedresser. 'Every branch in me that does not bear fruit He takes away; and every branch that bears fruit HE prunes, that it may bear more fruit. Abide in ME, and I in you. As the branch cannot bear fruit of itself, unless it abides in the vine, neither can you, unless you abide in ME. I am the vine, you are the branches. He who abides in ME, and I in him, bears much fruit; for without me you can do nothing.' "[3]

God is the gardener. Jesus is the vine. We are the branches. This is the only way fruit is produced. Children need to be told that the closer they follow God the greater their harvest.

---

1. Gal. 5.22-23; 2. Gen. 1.26; 3. John 15.1, 2, 4, 5.

# Guilt

Guilt is a state of mind that results from committing improper acts. To Christians, improper acts are those that break God's law. We feel guilty that we haven't lived up to God's standards.

Guilt can be good or bad. It's good when it helps people correct their behavior and bring them back to serving God joyfully. Bad guilt is destructive. It often results from following ungodly standards that paralyze the mind. It serves as a negative force in people's lives.

Children need to be taught there's no escape. The sooner they accept responsibility for their action the less severe the consequences and the sooner they will be relieved of much of the mental and physical anguish guilt produces. There is "Tribulation and anguish, on every soul of man who does evil . . ."[1]

Children should not feel guilty when they put forth their best effort and circumstances beyond their control cause them to fail. On the other hand, they should feel guilty, when they lie, cheat and break the law. None are more dangerous to themselves and others than those who break the law and do not have one tinge of guilt. It's important that guilt feelings get resolved; otherwise, negative consequences are sure to follow.

Guilt feelings are prompted by conscience: the inner voice which tells people whether their thoughts and actions are right or wrong. Shaping conscience in children is one of the most important responsibilities of parenting. They will grow up having or not having a conscience based on the moral values instilled in them especially during the pre-school years. What

45

children learn during this period will remain an active force in their lives as long as they live. Children's concept of right and wrong is formed, to a great extent, by the way parents train and instruct them and by the kinds of behavior parents accept or reject. For example, if parents are too strict in their childrearing, children may experience excessive or distorted guilt feelings. On the other hand if parents are too permissive, children may feel no guilt when they do wrong. This can cause them to be destructive and dangerous to others as well as themselves.

Parents who rely solely on their own knowledge during childrearing are bound to be found lacking. Those children raised by parents following God's standards for childrearing are much more likely to grow up with a healthy conscience. A guilt-ridden conscience cripples the mind! Children will feel good about themselves when they have acted responsibly and done right and irresponsible and confused when they have done wrong. "Fear (reverence) God and keep HIS commandments, for this is man's all."[2] "To the pure all things are pure, but to those who are defiled and unbelieving nothing is pure; but even their mind and conscience are defiled."[3] Children thrive and benefit most when they are guided by God's Law.

Children need not be burdened by guilt. In order for this to happen, however, they must first admit the sin that is causing the guilt. "He who covers his sins will not prosper, but whoever confesses and forsakes them will have mercy."[4] Unconfessed sin breeds guilt and guilt is at the root of most emotional and physical ailments. "If we confess our sins, He is faithful and just to forgive us our sins and to cleanse us from all unrighteousness."[5]

Second, children who have guilt feelings must correct their behavior. "Therefore, do not let sin reign in your mortal body ...."[6] This will rid their bodies of guilt.

Third, they must ask God to forgive them. "There is therefore now no condemnation to those who are in Christ Jesus, who do not walk according to the flesh, but according to the

Spirit.''⁷ Unconfessed guilt squeezes out Spiritual power that can rid emotional, mental and physical anguish sin brings on.

---

1. Rom. 2.9.; 2. Eccles. 12.13; 3. Titus 1.15; 4. Prov. 28.13; 5. 1 John 1.9; 6. Rom. 6.12; 7. Rom. 8.1.

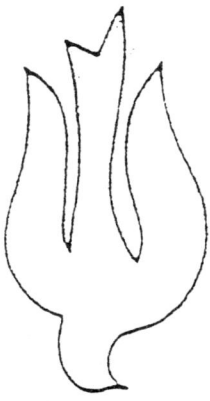

# Habits

Helping your children learn good habits is a valuable gift. Because once the bad ones have been established, they're terribly difficult to break. For example, children who develop poor eating habits not only add to their health problems, such as high cholesterol, but they will be faced with the difficult task of breaking those habits or suffer the consequences. Children's character and personality are greatly determined by their habits. There are hundreds of things children do everyday by habit. This frees them to focus on tasks and responsibilities that can't be done by habit. Children need and welcome a certain amount of routine in their lives. It makes them feel secure when there's a set pattern of activities they can count on.

One of the most important responsibilities of parenting is identifying good habits and teaching them to their children. They should include behavior such as:

1. good manners
2. personal hygiene
3. eating healthy food
4. not watching excessive TV
5. getting plenty of exercise
6. looking for the best in others

A few approaches parents can use to teach children good habits would include: setting a good example for them to follow; teach Bible principles by reading Bible stories to them until they are old enough to read the Bible on their own; help them select good playmates. "Do not be deceived: 'Evil company corrupts good habits.' "[1] "He who walks with wise men will be wise, but the companion of fools will be destroyed."[2]

Children are well on their way to living successfully when they are equipped with as many good habits as possible. They are happier, more confident, more independent, more responsible and they grow in self-worth. Good habits also contribute greatly to a more peaceful household and more enjoyable family living. A Spanish proverb says that habits are first cobwebs then cables!

---

1. 1 Cor. 15.33; 2. Prov. 13.20.

# Happiness

Happiness comes from within. It's an internal spiritual matter, joy in the knowledge of our salvation, rather than an external material one. Happiness is also related to how we react to life around us. Our purpose in life is not necessarily to be happy in all things but to behave responsibly by treating others kindly. Responsible behavior creates a sense of inner harmony and contentment that generates happiness. Truly happy people are those ". . . who walk in the law of the Lord!"[1] True happiness depends on our relationship with God.

Our pursuit of happiness is the driving force in most all we do. There are no limits to the sacrifices we make and the pain we endure to achieve it. We want it so much we spend our whole life in search of it.

Parents have to guard against giving children the impression that worldly values and not spiritual values are the key to happiness. Jesus said, " 'Do not lay up for yourselves treasures on earth, where moths and rust destroy and where thieves break in and steal; But lay up for yourselves treasures in heaven, where neither moth nor rust destroys and where thieves do not break in and steal. For where your treasure is, there your heart will be also.' ' "[2] It follows then that happy parents are much more likely to raise happy children.

There are many who have all the worldly possessions they could possibly have and still lack happiness. One of the most well known is King Solomon. In reflecting on his life he concluded that man's happiness is more of an internal matter than external: in the normal and healthy exercise of his powers of mind and body in harmony with the physical and moral laws of the universe in which he finds himself. Anything else is

"... grasping for the wind."[3] Many think "getting" is the way to happiness. The Bible teaches the exact opposite: "giving" is the key .... " 'It is more blessed to give than to receive.' "[4] Those who live by this principle confirm that it's true. Giving is loving. When we give, we control our happiness. We can be as happy as we are willing to give. Oddly enough, the more we give, the happier we become and the happier we become the more we have to give.

It is God's desire that we live happy lives. However, this can only be accomplished through faith, prayer and trust in God. "Happy is the man who finds wisdom, and the man who gains understanding."[5] "He has made everything beautiful in its time.... I know that nothing is better for them than to rejoice, and to do good in their lives; And also that every man should eat and drink and enjoy the good of his labor — it is a gift of God."[6]

Happiness is something people can decide to have in their lives now. They can be as happy as they choose to be. "This is the day the Lord has made; we will rejoice and be glad in it."[7] That means that this day is perfect. There is nothing else. The message to the believer is to be happy with what is there rather than be unhappy with what is not.

---

1. Ps. 119.1; 2. Matt. 6.19-21; 3. Eccles. 2.26; 4. Acts 20.35; 5. Prov. 3.13; 6. Eccles. 3.11-13; 7. Ps. 118.24.

# Heaven And Hell

Heaven is God's dwelling place. Children must learn that the Godly are destined for eternal life and shall forever be in God's presence. This is the hard road. " 'Narrow is the gate and difficult is the way which leads to life, and there are few who find it.' "[1] The narrow road leads to heaven. It is the place for those who accept, trust and obey God.

Hell is the place for those not in Christ. It means total separation from God. This is the easy road. " '... For wide is the gate and broad is the way that leads to destruction, and there are many who go in by it.' "[2] The broad road leads to Hell. It is the place reserved for those who disobey and reject God.

Heaven or Hell cannot be forced on people. All have the freedom to decide their own fate. People are free to choose the narrow road and serve God or, choose the broad road and serve self. There are only two groups of people in this world: those on their way to Heaven and those on their way to Hell. "... Choose for yourself this day whom you will serve ...."[3] There is no in between!

---

1. Matt. 7.14; 2. Matt. 7.13; 3. Josh. 24.15.

# Heredity And Environment

Children respond to their environment based to a great extent on their inherited characteristics. However, they should not be made to feel inferior or cheated because of hereditary differences. They have no control over it. They can't change it. And their worth as a human being should not depend on it. It's God's plan for them to be different. Therefore, they should not be compared to one another. When parents view their children in this light, they not only prevent them from feeling inferior or superior, they actually help them discover God's plan for their lives.

Since heredity is pre-determined there's little parents can do about it. But, they can do a lot about environment and this can make the biggest difference in how children turn out. One of the most critical factors in children's lives is their environment. At the moment of conception environment impacts on children physically, emotionally and mentally. It's up to parents to provide a good environment for their children. A healthy environment would include such things as:

1. providing safe conditions in which to grow up
2. adapting discipline to the individual child
3. spending as much time as possible with them
4. correcting them in a loving way
5. focusing on their strengths
6. instilling a positive attitude
7. "catching" them doing right
8. helping them acquire a healthy self-image
9. making children feel special
10. supplying healthy physical and spiritual food

Everything children experience in the environment is recorded in their minds — forever! The more caring the environment the better children will respond and thrive.

Children's minds at birth are like newly-plowed fields. What grows will be determined by the quality of the soil, the kind of seeds planted and the care given. These factors will determine the quality and quantity of fruit produced. Something is going to grow, if not seeds then weeds. Once the seeds are planted the kind of fruit won't change.

# Humility

Humility means being modest rather than showy. Humble people are admired and respected by all. People want to be around them. They aren't braggers. They're quick to listen and slow to speak. They live their lives according to God's will rather than their own. The Bible teaches that the humble will be exalted. "Humble yourselves in the sight of the Lord, and He will lift you up."[1]

Humility does not come naturally to children. They need to be taught by example more than by words. Children must be convinced that good things happen to those who live humble lives. God says, " 'If My people who are called by My name will humble themselves, and pray and seek My face, and turn from their wicked ways, then I will hear from heaven, and will forgive their sin and heal their land.' "[2] Practicing humility is one way of allowing God to work in our lives. Teaching children humility is difficult but not impossible.

---

1. James 4.10; 2. 2 Chr. 7.14.

# Jesus

Just before Jesus ascended to heaven, He instructed His handful of disciples to continue the work He had begun. " 'Go therefore and make disciples of all the nations, baptizing them in the name of the Father and of the Son and of the Holy Spirit, Teaching them to observe all things that I have commanded you.' "[1] The moral and spiritual values born out of His Word provide the foundation for sound character and good citizenship.

Jesus teaches the importance of forming a personal relationship with God. This means submitting to Him; putting God first in our lives. By example, parents have to teach their children how to nurture this relationship through prayer, study and obedience to His Word.

Based on human strength alone, this is impossible . . . . "But with God all things are possible."[2] Jesus told His disciples He would send them a helper. " 'But the Helper, the Holy Spirit, whom the father will send in My name, He will teach you all things.' "[2] The Holy Spirit is God's power which assures us "I can do all things through Christ who strengthens me."[4]

Jesus reveals HIMSELF in the following "I AM" statements:

1. ... " 'I am the bread of life. He who comes to ME shall never hunger, and he who believes in ME shall never thirst.' "[5]
2. ... " 'I am the light of the world. He who follows ME shall not walk in darkness, but have the light of life.' "[6]
3. " 'I am the door. If anyone enters by ME, he will be saved, and will go in and out and find pasture.' "[7]

4. " 'I am the good shepherd. The good shepherd gives HIS life for the sheep.' "[8]

5. ... " 'I am the resurrection and the life. He who believes in ME, though he may die, he shall live.' "[9]

6. ... " 'I am the way, the truth, and the life. No one comes to the Father except through ME.' "[10]

7. " 'I am the vine, you are the branches. He who abides in ME, and I in him, bears much fruit; for without ME you can do nothing.' "[11]

The following verses are from the Sermon on the Mount known as the Beatitudes. Jesus tells us what actions bring blessing, happiness and life as God intended:[12]

1. " 'Blessed are the poor in spirit, for theirs is the kingdom of heaven.' " The poor in spirit are humble. It means living according to God's will as opposed to our own, an awareness that we need God in our lives. Even though we may possess all things desirable in this world, they appear as nothing at death. How different life would be if we came to this understanding with time remaining so we could still do something about it.

2. " 'Blessed are those who mourn, for they shall be comforted.' " We will be blessed when we care so much about doing God's will that we experience grief and sorrow when it's not accomplished.

3. " 'Blessed are the meek, for they shall inherit the earth.' " Meek means to live our lives according to God's plan by submitting to His laws. Only then can God meet our needs. Meek people cheerfully submit to God's rule. They are not weak. They are strong and confident in the Lord!

4. " 'Blessed are those who hunger and thirst for righteousness, for they shall be filled.' " Those who have gone without food and water for even a short time know how strong the urge to satisfy these needs really is. Jesus tells us if we seek God's will with this same determination, we will surely come to know it and have it be a force in our lives.

5. " 'Blessed are the merciful, for they shall obtain mercy.' " Without mercy all of us are without hope. The

consideration, concern and compassion we expect from others, and more importantly from God are determined by the mercy we show toward others.

6. " 'Blessed are the pure in heart, for they shall see God.' " Being pure in heart means learning all about God to the best of our ability: loving God with all our heart, soul and mind. Then we will spiritually see God and know His kingdom in part now and totally in eternity. "For now we see in a mirror dimly, but then face to face. Now I know in part, but then I shall know just as I am known."[13]

7. " 'Blessed are the peacemakers, for they shall be called sons of God.' " Peacemakers promote harmony, friendship, unity and healing. Peacemaking has high priority in God's kingdom: peace with ourselves, with others and with God. Peace forces out fear, hate, and suspicion and replaces them with love, understanding and trust. If we have everything and lack peace of mind, it's as if we have nothing.

These seven Beatitudes reveal God's character and give us a glimpse of His Kingdom. Our time on earth serves as a training period for the life after. Life provides many opportunities to experience a bit of Heaven on earth. There is a price to pay, however. Being God's representative will not be easy. Jesus said many will " '... Say all kinds of evil against you falsely for My sake ....' "[14] " 'They will also persecute you ....' "[15] But, he says, " 'Rejoice and be exceedingly glad, for great is your reward in Heaven ....' "[16]

No person or event in recorded history comes even close to having the impact the birth, life, death and resurrection of Jesus had and continues to have in the world. His appearance on earth divided time into two periods: all that happened BEFORE CHRIST (BC) and all that happened since, ANNO DOMINI (AD) in the year of the Lord. Jesus The Christ is the central figure in all of history and creation.

**"One Solitary Life"** ... "Here is a young man who was born in an obscure village, the child of a peasant woman. He grew up in another village. He worked in a carpenter shop until He was thirty, and then for three years He was an itinerant preacher. He never wrote a book. He never held an office. He never owned a home. He never had a family. He never went to college. He never put his foot inside a big city. He never traveled more than 200 miles from the place where he was born. He never did one of the things that accompany greatness. He had no credentials but himself.

"While He was still a young man, the tide of public opinion turned against Him. His friends ran away. He was turned over to His enemies. He went through the mockery of a trial, He was nailed to a cross between two thieves. While He was dying, His executioners gambled for the only piece of property He had on earth, and that was His coat. When He was dead, He was laid in a borrowed grave through the pity of a friend.

"Nineteen centuries have come and gone, and today He is the central figure of the human race and the leader of the column of progress. I am far within the mark when I say that all the armies that ever marched, and all the navies that ever sailed, and all the governments that ever sat, and all the kings that ever reigned, put together, have not affected the life of man upon this earth as has that One Solitary Life." (Anonymous)

It's unfortunate that children in America don't know at least as much about Jesus as they do about George Washington. Jesus was without sin and His sole purpose is to help each and every person become reconciled to God. Developing God-like character assures each person of the gift of eternal life. " '... He who believes in Me, though he may die, he shall live.' " [17] This is the purpose of human existence. Jesus is the role model not only for parents but the entire human race.

---

1. Matt. 28.19, 20; 2. Matt. 19.26; 3. John 14.26; 4. Phil. 4.13; 5. John 6.35; 6. John 8.12; 7. John 10.9; 8. John 10.11; 9. John 11.25; 10. John 14.6; 11. John 15.5; 12. Matt. 5.3-9; 13. 1 Cor. 13.12; 14. Matt. 5.11; 15. John. 15.20; 16. Matt. 5.12; 17. John 11.25.

# Judging

Judging must be left to God. He is just. He is the final authority. Jesus tells us to, " 'Judge not, that you be not judged. For with what judgment you judge, you will be judged; and with the measure you use, it will be measured back to you. And why do you look at the speck in your brother's eye, but do not consider the plank in your own eye? Or how can you say to your brother, Let me remove the speck from your eye; and look, a plank is in your own eye? Hypocrite! First remove the plank from your own eye, and then you will see clearly to remove the speck from your brother's eye.' "[1] This means we are not to condemn others regardless of their weaknesses and shortcomings.

People who judge others often do it to make themselves look better at the expense of others. God says to hate the sin but love the sinner, regardless of the nature of the sin. It's to be left to God to separate right from wrong. He " 'will render to each one according to his deeds.' "[2] " 'For by your words you will be justified, and by your words you will be condemned.' "[3] He will do this in His own time. All have sinned. All come short of the Glory of God. None achieve perfection in this life.

When the scribes and Pharisees pressed Jesus to pass judgment on the woman taken in adultery, Jesus responded in the following way: " '. . . He who is without sin among you, let him throw a stone at her first.' When Jesus had raised Himself up and saw no one but the woman, He said to her, 'Woman, where are those accusers of yours? Has no one condemned you?' She said, 'No one, Lord.' And Jesus said to her, 'Neither do I condemn you; go and sin no more.' "[4] When children give other children the opportunity to learn, grow and change rather than condemn, they benefit themselves as well as others. " 'Judge not, and you shall not be judged. Condemn not, and you shall not be condemned. Forgive, and you will be forgiven.' "[5] Children need to understand that their rewards and punishment in this life and the lifeafter will be based on their conduct and performance in this life.

*"There is so much good in the worst of us,*
*and so much bad in the best of us,*
*That it hardly becomes any of us*
*To talk about the rest of us." Author unknown*

---

1. Matt. 7.1-5; 2. Rom. 2.6; 3. Matt. 12.37; 4. John 8.7, 10, 11; 5. Luke 6.37.

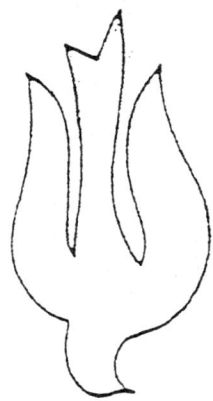

# Judgment

The day is coming when we will be judged. Why not be prepared? Children need to know that each of them will face a judgment day. "And as it is appointed for men to die once, but after this the judgment."[1] " 'Therefore I will judge you, . . . every one according to his ways.' "[2] "And I saw the dead, small and great, standing before God, and books were opened. And another book was opened, which is the book of Life. And the dead were judged according to their works, by the things which were written in the book. The sea gave up the dead who were in it, and death and Hades (grave) delivered up the dead who were in them. And they were judged each one according to his works."[3] Abraham calls God "The judge of all the earth."[4] He may delay judgment but He will do it at the right time, in the right way. God judges according to what people have done with their lives.

One way parents can help their children prepare for their judgment day is by sharing the Spiritual concepts they acquire from their spiritual birth, such as:

1. SAVIOR — " 'For God did not send His Son into the world to condemn the world, but that the world through Him might be saved.' "[5]

2. GRACE — "For by grace you have been saved through faith, and that not of yourselves; it is the gift of God."[6]

3. FORGIVENESS — "But if we walk in the light as He is in the light, we have fellowship with one another, and the blood of Jesus Christ His Son cleanses us from all sin."[7]

4. HELP — " 'Come to me, all you who labor and are heavy laden, and I will give you rest.' "[8]

5. PEACE — "And the peace of God, which surpasses all understanding, will guard your hearts and minds through Christ Jesus."[9]

6. HOPE — "For I consider that the sufferings of this present time are not worthy to be compared with the glory which shall be revealed in us."[10]

7. ETERNAL LIFE — "For the wages of sin is death, but the gift of God is eternal life in Christ Jesus our Lord."[11]

We can be joyful as we understand our lives through the life, death and resurrection of Jesus. For those who believe, there is no cause for fear. God will receive them as His own.

---

1. Heb. 9.27; 2. Ezek. 18.30; 3. Rev. 20.12, 13; 4. Gen. 18.25; 5. John 3.17; 6. Eph. 2.8; 7. 1 John 1.7; 8. Matt. 11.28; 9. Phil. 4.7; 10. Rom. 8.18; 11. Rom. 6.23.

# Love

Children need to know about the different kinds of love: first the love of God. "... God is love, and he who abides in love abides in God, and God in him.[1] In this the love of God was manifested toward us, that God has sent His only begotten Son into the world, that we might live through Him. In this is love, not that we loved God, but that He loved us and sent His Son to be the propitiation (atoning sacrifice) for our sins.[2] We love Him because He first loved us."[3] " 'Greater love has no one than this, than to lay down one's life for his friends.' "[4]

God's love is unconditional. He does not withhold His love because people are sinful. When Jesus was asked which is the great commandment in the law He said, ... " 'You shall love the Lord your God with all your heart, with all your mind. This is the first and great commandment.' "[5]

The second kind of love is love for others. "Love suffers long and is kind; love does not envy; love does not parade itself, is not puffed up; Does not behave rudely, does not seek its own, is not provoked, thinks no evil; Does not rejoice in iniquity (evil) but rejoices in the truth; Bears all things, believes all things, hopes all things, endures all things. Love never fails."[6] This is divine love. It is something for all to strive towards. " 'If you can believe, all things are possible to him who believes.' "[7]

Genuine Christian love is much more than emotion. It involves both mind and will. It's obedience to God's second great commandment. " '... You shall love your neighbor as yourself (neighbor is anyone who provides us with an opportunity to serve). On these two commandments hang all the Law and

64

the Prophets.' "[8] Parents need to so instruct their children so that they love, respect and understand themselves as well as others. " ... If God so loved us, we also ought to love one another."[9] "... He who does not love his brother whom he has seen, how can he love God whom he has not seen?"[10] " 'And above all things have fervent love for one another, for love will cover a multitude of sins.' "[11]

Jesus laid down His life for everybody. This should inspire children to give of themselves for another because true love is truly sacrificial. Love means to do what is right regardless of the cost and actually rejoice in the good fortunes of others. Not only are we to love our neighbors, Jesus said, " 'I say to you, love your enemies, bless those who curse you, do good to those who hate you, and pray for those who spitefully use you and persecute you.' "[12] God's love always means to seek the highest good for others, no matter what they may have done or not done. This is what He did.

Children need to be loved if they are to grow up to be loving. They need love, security and acceptance from the very beginning. They need praise, encouragement and instruction more than correction even when they are not very loving. This message can be transmitted in various ways:

1. accept them for what they are and not for what we wish they were
2. show them affection including physical contact
3. answer their questions and praise them
4. show genuine interest; children believe the things parents say about them
5. pay as close attention to their spiritual food as their physical food
6. compare them only with themselves
7. tell them you love them
8. discipline them privately; public embarrassment strips them of their dignity
9. play with them
10. give them a reasonable amount of individual attention
11. forgive and forget their mistakes

Children don't belong to parents, they belong to God. Children who experience a shortage of happiness adopt values that perpetuate that unhappiness in later life. Children should be encouraged to love others so genuinely that at times they can even put others ahead of themselves without feeling resentful. The Bible teaches that we are to love others at least as much as we love ourselves.

We discover deeper meaning and purpose to life not in search of self but rather in surrender of self to obedience to Christ. When the mind is full of God's love, there is no room for worry, hate, fear and all the other emotional states that tear people down rather than build them up as God would have us do. All stand to benefit from love — those who receive it as well as those who extend it.

---

1. 1 John 4.16; 2. 1 John 4.9, 10; 3. 1 John 4.19; 4. John 15.13; 5. Matt. 22.37, 38; 6. 1 Cor. 13.4-8; 7. Mark 9.23; 8. Matt. 22.39, 40; 9. 1 John 4.11; 10. 1 John 4.20; 11. 1 Pet. 4.8; 12. Matt. 5.44.

# Marriage

Children learn about marriage from their parents. This begins very early in life. They use their parents' marriage as a model. This is what they take with them to their marriage and pass on to their children. They should be exposed to the struggles as well as the successes. Their expectations need to be realistic. Somehow the message that marriage is not all fun and games doesn't get through. They need to know that all households have their share of sadness and joy. Parents should not hesitate to discuss these matters at the appropriate time. Many opportunities to do this will arise naturally such as at meal times, weddings, funerals, reunions and hundreds of other occasions. Discussing the Christian marriage with children helps prepare them for the event in their own lives.

In the beginning God established the marriage bond. " '... Have you not read that He who made them at the beginning made them male and female.' And said, 'For this reason a man shall leave his father and mother and be joined to his wife, and the two shall become one flesh.' "[1] Marriage is the most intimate relationship; and it was designed to be one of the most fulfilling and rewarding. For this to be true, however, Biblical principles pertaining to marriage must be followed. "Unless the Lord builds the house, they labor in vain who build it ...."[2] Marriage is not a human invention; it is God's creation.

For marriage to be what God intended, He has to be at the center. My way and your way are replaced with His way: looking upward rather than inward. "Submitting to one another in the fear (reverence) of God."[3] Mutually submitting to one another and to God means husbands and wives are able to consider the needs of the other as more important than their own. To do this they keep God at the center of their marriage and submit to His teachings. When their fragile support lines intertwine with Him they form an unbreakable cord. "And a threefold cord is not quickly broken."[4] Since all husbands and wives are imperfect, they should not expect perfection in their marriage. Only God is perfect. This is why with God at the center of the marriage, all things become manageable.

One of the most important factors in marriage is choosing the right partner. The Bible is very specific about this. "Do not be unequally yoked together with unbelievers . . . ."[5] This means the marriage will be built using two different sets of blueprints. Being equally yoked means using the same set of blueprints to build the marriage. Neither will be built without hard work. But which one is likely to encounter more problems? The most important ingredient of a good and happy Christian marriage is that husband and wife share a common faith and belief in God. Though this doesn't guarantee a good marriage, couples who do not share a common faith are more likely to experience difficulties in marriage. Children need to be made aware of this information even though they may choose to ignore it when they select their marriage partner.

Children also need to be aware of the differences between husbands and wives. God said, " 'Let us make man in our image, according to Our likeness . . . .' So God created man in His own image; in the image of God He created him; male and female He created them."[6] God meant each of them to be unique. Though they differ physically, mentally, emotionally and may have different gifts, they are all of equal value and importance in God's eyes. God didn't put all strengths of character in one sex. The differing masculine and feminine gifts and talents are to be mutually respected and appreciated. They are intended to complement, not battle against each other, especially husbands and wives. This understanding is not only essential for a good marriage, it provides a solid sex identity model for healthy childrearing by doing such things as:

1. trying to see the other's point of view
2. resolving conflicts as soon as possible
3. being as forgiving as possible
4. asking what he or she can do to help
5. trying to maintain a prayerful attitude
6. learning to be the person God wants him or her to be
7. avoiding blame because it only makes matters worse
8. treating each other as he or she would want to be treated

Remember, it's important that you serve as a good role model for your children. They'll be watching!

---

1. Matt. 19.4, 5; 2. Ps. 127.1; 3. Eph. 5.21; 4. Eccles. 4.12; 5. 2 Cor. 6.14; 6. Gen. 1.26, 27.

# Mistakes

"Hindsight is 20/20," someone once said. So when our children make mistakes, let's help them learn from them. Making mistakes is part of being human. No one is free of them. "For we all stumble in many things."[1] Children learn more from their mistakes than any other method of learning.

Parents should not make children feel fearful of making mistakes. In fact mistakes provide opportunities for them to find better ways of doing things. Good parenting welcomes mistakes because children learn so much from them. Parents need to encourage their children to learn from their mistakes then forget them.

Children learn much from risk-taking, as long as they are not life-threatening. They instill confidence, improve decision making, help children deal with uncertainties and most importantly, help them develop healthy self-images so necessary for success in school and in life. "Far better is to dare mighty things, to win glorious triumphs, even though checkered by failure, than to take rank with those poor spirits who neither enjoy much nor suffer much, because they live in the gray twilight that knows not victory nor defeat," said Theodore Roosevelt.

Children think parents know everything. We know different. Our mistakes shouldn't be hidden for they can be learning opportunities too.

Children need to realize that God will not reprimand them for making honest mistakes, especially when they seek His guidance and direction. They need to be told that He promises to forgive and forget all their mistakes when they admit them, accept responsibility for them, do not repeat them, and ask God's forgiveness.

---

1. James 3.2.

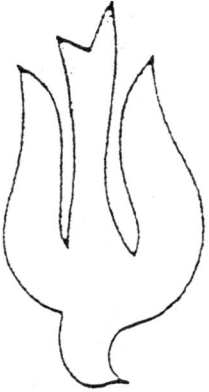

# Money

Parents need to teach their children the value of money as early as possible. They should be allowed to make as many purchases as possible with the money allotted them and live with mistakes and mismanagement — the price of learning. They should be encouraged to save some of their money to buy more expensive things later. At some point, probably after they have started school, give them an allowance so they can pay for needed items. They must learn to distinguish between needs and wants and practice the principle of using it up, making it do and wearing it out. It is never too early to encourage giving to charity and savings. As they get older, encourage them to get a part-time job and open a savings account. As difficult as it may seem at times, the more parents persist the more likely children will establish wise saving and spending habits that will last a lifetime.

# Morality

Moral laws spell out right and wrong behavior. Ethics is the process by which these determinations are made. For the Christian, the process is always God-centered instead of self-centered. "There is a way which seems right to a man, but its end is the way of death."[1] Living a moral life means being in harmony with God. Just as following natural laws protect children from physical harm, following spiritual laws shields them from much of life's sufferings and helps them through unavoidable difficulties.

Children need moral standards by which they can make behavioral choices. God's word provides them with those standards. Parents who rear their children by God's laws can do so with the assurance that they will serve them throughout life because "Jesus Christ is the same yesterday, today, and forever."[2] This is not the case with those who make their own rules. . . "" I have set before you life and death, blessings and cursing (suffering); therefore choose life, that both you and your descendants may live."[3]

Children will not always be easily convinced that God's morality is in their best interest. Children need to be reminded "... That all things work together for good to those who love God, to those who are called according to His purpose."[4]

God holds parents responsible for teaching their children right from wrong. "And these words which I command you this day shall be in your heart. You shall teach them diligently to your children, and shall talk of them when you sit in your house, when you walk by the way, when you lie down, and when you rise up."[5] Children instilled with a moral code of ethics grounded in the Bible will be well equipped to make all the right moral choices life will require of them. Every moral principle not followed will result in negative consequences for children, parents and probably others as well. "Call to Me, and I will answer you, and show you great and mighty things, which you do not know."[6]

---

1. Prov. 14.12; 2. Heb. 13.8; 3. Deut. 30.19; 4. Rom. 8.28; 5. Deut. 6.6-7; 6. Jer. 33.3.

# Motives

Motives dictate our actions. They are the reason people do what they do. It may be to impress others. It may be for personal recognition and gain or fear of certain consequences. Whatever the case, God knows what it is. "All the ways of a man are pure in his own eyes, but the Lord weighs the spirits (motives)."[1] ". . . For the Lord does not see as man sees; for man looks at the outward appearance, but the Lord looks at the heart."[2] Motives play a very important part in life. Doing something for the wrong reason can be a haunting experience. It can turn out to be a source of serious resentment and great disappointment.

Children need to be taught that God knows what they are thinking before they do. "For the ways of man are before the eyes of the Lord, and He ponders (examines) all his paths."[3] "... For the Lord searches all hearts and understands all the intent of the thoughts ...."[4] Children often think they can fool their brothers, sisters, parents, friends and teachers but they cannot fool God. They will soon learn they only fool themselves.

The Bible teaches that God should be the source of our motivation. Children need to be taught to live as Jesus lived. "Let this mind be in you which was also in Christ Jesus."[5] God knows when they are doing their best and that is all He expects of them. Their actions are to please God first rather than themselves or others. " 'But when you do a charitable deed, do not let your left hand know what your right hand is doing, That your charitable deed may be in secret; and your Father who sees in secret will Himself reward you openly.' "[6] Unfortunately, people's actions are often based on what people think rather than on what God thinks. Doing something because it is right is not enough. They insist on the recognition and credit from others as well.

There is no telling how much good could be accomplished in this world if individuals focused on pleasing God rather than people. " 'Take heed that you do not do your charitable deeds before men, to be seen by them. Otherwise you have no reward from your Father in heaven.' "[7] "Let nothing be done through selfish ambition or conceit ...."[8] Only that which is done for the glory of God will merit His glory and reward.

---

1. Prov. 16.2; 2. 1 Sam. 16.7; 3. Prov. 5.21; 4. 1 Chr. 28.9; 5. Phil. 2.5; 6. Matt. 6.3, 4; 7. Matt. 6.1; 8. Phil. 2.3.

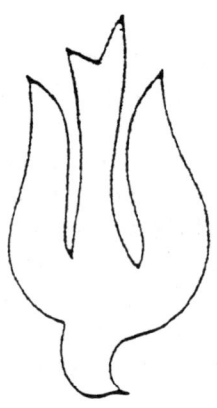

# Neighbors

The Bible definition of neighbor is found in Luke's gospel. When Jesus was asked by a lawyer "who is my neighbor?" He answered his question with the well-known Good Samaritan parable. A man was wounded, robbed and left for dead. He was ignored by two "God-fearing" people. The third person, a heathen, took care of him in a manner he would have wanted to be treated. Then Jesus asked, "So which of these three do you think was neighbor to him who fell among the thieves?" And he said, 'he who showed mercy on him.' Then Jesus said to him, 'go and do likewise.' "[1]

Since "... God created man in His own image, ..."[2] each and every human being is of equal value and importance to Him. Children need to be taught to see others in this perspective. Nothing pleases parents more than when others treat their children kindly. God feels the same way. It means wishing and wanting what's best for others. "For all the law is fulfilled in one word, even this: 'you shall love your neighbor as yourself.' "[3] " 'Therefore, whatever you want men to do to you, do also to them ....' "[4]

Children will be held accountable for their behavior towards others, based on their maturity level. It may help to remind them that they will see their neighbors in eternity. When children focus on others instead of themselves, it not only benefits others, it transforms their lives as well.

Children need to understand that loving their neighbor means practicing Biblical principles such as:

1. Loving others in spite of their faults. God does!
2. Their words should lighten the burdens of others.
3. Building others up rather than tearing them down.

4. Forgiving others and being kind.
5. Considering the need of others at least as important as their own.
6. Loving others as God loves them.
7. Living God-fearing (reverent) lives.
8. Acting in ways that attract rather than drive others away.
9. Treating others as equals.

Even though children may not understand or actually live by these principles, parents should continue to teach them by their words and more importantly, by example. "Let each of you look out not only for his own interests, but also for the interests of others."[5] "... All of you be of one mind, having compassion for one another; love as brothers, be tenderhearted, be courteous; Not returning evil for evil or reviling (insults) for reviling, but on the contrary blessing, knowing that you were called to this, that you may inherit a blessing."[6]

---

1. Luke 10.36-37; 2. Gen. 1.27; 3. Gal. 5.14; 4. Matt. 7.12; 5. Phil. 2.4; 6. 1 Pet. 3.8-9.

# Obedience

Don't you wish your kids were more obedient? Well God says the same thing about us! We are to obey the Lord. And children are to obey their parents. "Children, obey your parents in the Lord, for this is right."[1] Because people of all ages are more self-centered than God-centered, there's natural resistance to obedience.

Teaching obedience must begin early. Children learn more about it during the first few years of life than any other time. They have to be taught to obey long before they are able to reason why. Table behavior, coming when called, and respect for adults and other children is a good place to start. Unless children learn to respect and obey their parents, they will not respect and obey their teacher, established rules, the law and their future employer. Of course, expectations must be in line with children's capabilities. "Fathers (mothers) do not provoke your children, lest they become discouraged."[2]

Children learn disobedience when parents do not follow up on what they say. Telling them to obey will not always make it happen. Children must be shown, boundaries defined, impossible demands avoided. Reminders should be kind, loving and patient. Parents should not expect obedience in every instance; allow for misunderstandings. Overlook minor infractions. Focus on important issues. Catch children at doing right rather than wrong and tell them and others about it.

Parents who really love their children do not ignore inappropriate behavior. Disobedient children feel confused, frustrated and unloved. They are miserable and make others miserable. Obedience has not been established by God to keep us from enjoying life. God has commanded it because He knows that the greatest freedom, strength, power and fulfill-ment is in doing His will: doing right rather than engaging in wrong. " 'If you love Me, keep My commandments.' "[3]

---

1. Eph. 6.1; 2. Col. 3.21; 3. John 14.15.

# Patience

Patience is the ability to calmly endure unpleasant situations. Exercising self-control under trying circumstances presents the greatest challenge of all. "... Count it all joy when you fall into various trials, knowing that the testing of your faith produces patience."[1] Being patient means looking beyond present circumstances. We are to dwell on the fact that God is in charge rather than on complaining. "Rest in the Lord, and wait patiently for Him."[2] And, "I waited patiently for the Lord; and He inclined to me, and heard my cry."[3]

Parents should do everything possible to cultivate patience in their children. The reason it's so important is that impatience is the cause of most unhappiness. Patience should be encouraged when children's wants, needs and goals are not met immediately. They need to be reminded that each minute, hour and day that passes brings them closer to the end result.

Immaturity is the source of much discouragement. It is very hard for children to watch, wait and trust in God's wisdom working in their lives. "Teach me, O Lord, the way of your statutes, and I shall keep it to the ends."[4] "The Lord is good to those who wait for Him, to the soul who seeks Him."[5]

Children should be reminded that their problems during their lives on earth represent but a moment in time compared to eternity. "... Do not forget this one thing, that with the Lord one day is as a thousand years, and a thousand years as one day."[6] "And let us not grow weary while doing good, for in due season we shall reap if we do not lose heart."[7]

Patient people make the most of their trying times. They maintain a positive outlook. They seek ways to improve the situation. They think of ways to use the waiting time profitably.

Patience promotes peace of mind, good health and more importantly, glorifies God. Parents need to make every effort possible to instruct their children in the Godly trait of patience. "For you have need of endurance (patience) so that after you have done the will of God, you may receive the promise."[8]

1. James 1.2, 3; 2. Ps. 37.7; 3. Ps. 40.1; 4. Ps. 119.33; 5. Lam. 3.25; 6. 2 Pet. 3.8; 7. Gal. 6.9; 8. Heb. 10.36.

# Praise

Praise is a very important part of worshipping God and in raising children. The Bible places great emphasis on the importance of expressing praise and thankfulness. "I will bless the Lord at all times; His praise shall continually be in my mouth."[1] ". . . Let us continually offer the sacrifice of praise to God, that is, the fruit of our lips, giving thanks to His name."[2] "Anxiety in the heart of man causes depression, but a good word makes it glad."[3] "In everything give thanks; for this is the will of God in Christ Jesus for you."[4] When children understand the extent of God's love as revealed in Christ who lived, suffered, died for their salvation and rose again, praising God first and then praising others will come naturally.

Praise is such an important ingredient of successful parenting. It is much more effective in bringing out the best in children than criticism. "Pleasant words are like honeycomb, sweetness to the soul and health to the bones."[5] "Do not withhold good from those to whom it is due, when it is in the power of your hand to do so."[6]

Praise can work wonders. Parents should not just think praise; they should express it in their words and actions. How else can children know and benefit from it? Praise encourages, instills confidence and has the power to lift children's spirits so they can focus on all the positive aspects of their lives. "A word fitly spoken is like apples of gold in settings of silver."[7]

Praise should greatly outnumber criticism. Criticism reduces self-confidence, so necessary for future success.

Sincere praise increases it. Praise, encouragement and appreciation are needed by all. Everybody can be praised for something.

---

1. Ps. 34.1; 2. Heb. 13.15; 3. Prov. 12.25; 4. 1 Thess. 5.18; 5. Prov. 16.24; 6. Prov. 3.27; 7. Prov. 25.11.

# Prayer

Prayer is more than talking with God. It's spending time with Him, seeking to know His will, learning from Him, trying to be like Him.

The prophet Daniel, one of the greatest of God's spokesmen, teaches the importance of prayer. "... He knelt down on his knees three times that day, and prayed and gave thanks before his God, as was his custom since early days."[1] Prayer was his highest expression of reverence, devotion, obedience and praise of God.

Children need to be taught why prayer is important. First, God invites them to pray. "Call upon me in the day of trouble; I will deliver you, and you shall glorify Me."[2] He will not eliminate their trouble but will help them through it. Second, God is near them wherever they pray to Him. He promises to hear their prayers. " 'Ask, and it will be given to you; seek, and you will find; knock, and it will be opened to you.' "[3] Third, they should give thanks and praise to God in prayer. This means they should pray as Jesus did: that their lives will glorify God. " ... Whatever you do, do all to the glory of God."[4] This is not an easy task for anyone, especially children. The following passage speaks to this point. "I can do all things through Christ who strengthens me."[5] Through prayer children soon learn problems that seem overwhelming can become manageable. With prayer comes confidence, power "And the peace of God, which surpasses (exceeds) all understanding ...."[6]

Children need to be taught how to pray. Jesus gave us a model to follow when praying. In this manner, therefore, pray:[7]

1. **Our Father in heaven:** Jesus always prayed to the Father. Children are to approach God in the same way they approach their parents. " ... Give thanks to the Lord! Call upon His name ...."[8]

2. **Hallowed (holy) be your name:** They are to worship, honor and praise Him with their thoughts, words and deeds. "For the Lord is great and greatly to be praised ...."[9]

3. **Your Kingdom come:** Children are to do everything possible to live a godly life and represent His kingdom on earth. When Jesus was asked when the kingdom of God would come, He said, " 'For, indeed, the kingdom of God is within you.' "[10]

4. **Your will be done on earth as it is in heaven:** They need to ask God to help them understand what His will is and how to live it so that their lives will reflect His will. " 'Therefore I say to you, whatever things you ask when you pray, believe that you receive them, and you will have them.' "[11] God promises to answer prayers offered in His name.

5. **Give us this day our daily bread:** It's important that children understand that this passage refers to needs (physical as well as spiritual) and not their wants. Also, it means to admit they are totally dependent on God in much the same way that they are dependent on their parents. "Be anxious for nothing, but in everything by prayer and supplication (appeal), with thanksgiving, present your requests to God."[12] God knows of their needs even before they ask Him.

6. **And forgive us our debts (sins) as we forgive our debtors (those who sin against us):** Everyone sins so everyone needs to be forgiven. This passage states God will forgive them as they forgive others. " 'But if you do not forgive, neither will your Father in heaven forgive your trespasses.' "[12] When Jesus was asked how many times people should forgive, He replied, " '... I do not say to you, up to seven times, but up to seventy times seven.' "[14]

7. **And do not lead us into temptation:** God tempts no one to sin. They are asking God for strength to resist the temptations to do wrong. " '... Pray that you may not enter into temptation.' "[15]

8. **But deliver us from the evil one:** They are asking God to strengthen them spiritually so they may avoid and reject pitfalls they will encounter in life. This, of course, will not be easy. But, Jesus says, "Now this is the confidence that we have in Him, that if we ask anything according to His will, He hears us."[16]

9. **For yours is the kingdom and the power and the glory forever:** God's kingdom will prevail on earth as well as in heaven. " 'Blessed be the name of God forever and ever, for wisdom and might are His.' "[17] They can be part of it by trusting in His will and not their own.

**Amen.** It shall be so.

Just as prayer begins with reverence, love and praise, it should conclude the same way. Children should be encouraged to express gratitude for their countless blessings. They can always find something to be grateful for. They can learn to pray at mealtime, bedtime, during family devotions, church and on their own.

The sooner parents begin praying with their children, the more natural it will be for them as well as their children. They will soon discover the comfort that comes from sharing their fears and concerns with a loving God. He encourages them to bring their needs to Him faithfully and gain courage and power in His love. All through His ministry Jesus spent much time in prayer with God. He encourages us to do the same.

---

1. Dan. 6.10; 2. Ps. 50.15; 3. Matt. 7.7; 4. 1 Cor. 10.31; 5. Phil. 4.13; 6. Phil. 4.7; 7. Matt. 6.9-13; 8. 1 Chr. 16.8; 9. 1 Chr. 16.2; 10. Luke 17.21; 11. Mark 11.24; 12. Phil. 4.6; 13. Mark 11.26; 14. Matt. 18.22; 15. Luke 22.40; 16. 1 John 5.14; 17. Dan. 2.20.

# Pride

Pride is original sin. It is the first of the "seven" deadly sins. It is number one because it leads to every other sin. It is a way of thinking that puts self first and God second. Pride means we deny the true God and appoint ourselves as God. This allows us to put ourselves before others and do whatever is necessary for personal gain at any cost.

Pride destroys. "Pride goes before destruction, and a haughty (arrogant) spirit before a fall."[1] "The Lord will destroy the house of the proud."[2] Recall what happens to King Nebuchadnezzar: ". . . He was walking about the royal palace of Babylon," he said, 'Is not this the great Babylon I have built for a royal residence, by my mighty power and for the honor of my majesty?' While the word was still in the King's mouth, a voice came from heaven: 'King Nebuchadnezzer, to you it is spoken the kingdom has departed from you! And they shall drive you from men, and your dwelling shall be with the beast of the field. They shall make you eat grass like oxen.' "[3] Kings do not have a monopoly on pride. It can get a grip on anyone who pushes God out of his or her life.

The challenge for parents, then, is how to help their children avoid the pit of pride. The psalmist says: "Trust in the Lord with all your heart and lean not on your own understanding; In all your ways acknowledge Him, and He will make your paths straight."[4] Children need to conduct themselves according to what is acceptable to God not self.

Pride offends God because it degrades individuals who are equally important to Him. Children need to understand that God wants them to build others up not tear them down. Parents need to show consideration for others and teach their children to do the same. " '. . . God resists the proud but gives grace to the humble.' "[5] The less proud they are the more they will be able to follow God's will.

---

1. Prov. 16.18; 2. Prov. 15.25; 3. Dan. 4.29-32; 4. Prov. 3:5, 6; 5. 1 Pet. 5.5.

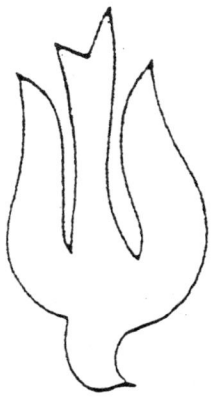

# Procrastination

Procrastination is needless delay. It's a weakness in our character which prevents us from doing what needs to be done. Often it's something people choose to avoid or escape from because it's distasteful. They tell themselves they'll do it later. Laziness is also part of the problem. Procrastination is a sinful human failing few escape totally.

Anything parents can do to minimize procrastination in their children will reap great dividends in their later years. The most unfortunate thing about this habit is all the time that is wasted. Over time, it robs children of their self-respect, mental health, new opportunities and time that could be devoted to many other useful activities.

A most serious postponement could be putting off coming to know Christ and His gift of salvation. "For not the hearers of the law are just in the sight of God, but the doers of the law who will be justified."[1] "Behold now is the accepted time; behold, now is the day of salvation."[2]

Overcoming procrastination is not easy. It leaves a trail of unfinished business wherever it goes. Attempts to justify it include making excuses, apologies and regrets. People who accomplish much good in their lives can serve as inspiration. They have dealt with the problem and this is what allows them to get so much done. Impressing upon children the importance of time is a good place to begin. "So teach us to number our days, that we may gain a heart of wisdom."[3]

Certain opportunities may occur only once in a lifetime. If they are not seized at that point, they may be lost forever. The odds of this happening with the procrastinator are much greater. Children need to be reminded of God's expectations of them. "And whatever you do, do it heartily, as to the Lord and not to men, Knowing that from the Lord you will receive the reward of the inheritance; for you serve the Lord Christ."[4]

---

1. Rom. 2.13; 2. 2 Cor. 6.2; 3. Ps. 90.12; 4. Col. 3.23, 24.

# Reading

Parents should be selective in what they allow children to read. There are plenty of good books available; but they are harder to find. Reading good books helps children:
1. Build vocabulary and speaking skills.
2. Encourage curiosity and imagination.
3. Develop thinking and reasoning.
4. Sharpen their listening skills.
5. Improve concentration span.
6. Recognize good writing.
7. Absorb abstract ideas.
8. Broaden their horizons.
9. Stimulate learning.
10. Acquire knowledge.
11. Learn how to learn.
12. Succeed in school and life.

When parents devote about 10 or 15 minutes a day reading aloud to their children they not only achieve the above, but the personal attention tells them they are valued, appreciated and loved.

Don't forget to read the books of the Bible! It is by far the most important collection of books ever written. "All Scripture is given by inspiration of God, and is profitable for doctrine, for reproof, for correction, for instruction in righteousness."[1] It is the true word of God and His way of speaking directly to each and every person. " 'For God so loved the world that He gave His only begotten Son, that whoever believes in Him should not perish but have everlasting life.' "[2] Salvation is the most important message in the whole Bible, along with explaining the meaning of life and hope for the future. A good children's Bible can make the reading easier to understand.

Parents need to impress upon their children, by example, that the Bible is first on the reading list. People could read every book written and still be ignorant; but if they only read the Bible they would be wise. Given the choice, people can get by not having read other books but they wouldn't want to live their lives without knowing about their salvation as revealed in the Bible.

Good reading habits are much more likely to take root in children when reading is an important part of their upbringing. The desire to read, like other meaningful accomplishments must come from within. Only then will children like it, pursue it and want to do more of it.

---

1. 2. Tim. 3.16; 2. John 3.16.

# Resurrection

Parents need to inform their children about God's promises about eternal life. "But I do not want you to be ignorant, brethren, concerning those who have fallen asleep, lest you sorrow as others who have no hope. For if we believe that Jesus died and rose again, even so God will bring with Him those who sleep in Jesus. For this we say to you by the word of the Lord, that we who are alive and remain until the coming of the Lord will by no means precede those who are asleep. For the Lord Himself will descend from heaven with a shout, with the voice of an archangel, and with the trumpet of God. And the dead in Christ will rise first. Then we who are alive and remain shall be caught up together with them in the clouds to meet the Lord in the air. And thus we shall always be with the Lord. Therefore comfort one another with these words."[1]

Children should know that their loved ones who have died in the faith will continue to live. That they too, who are alive in Christ will live and that all people who live and die in Christ will live.

The day will come when each one of us will have to give account of our lives. Parents need to see that their children know about and understand what the resurrection means for them. Jesus said, ". . . I am the resurrection and the life. He who believes in Me though he may die, he shall live."[2] This knowledge and understanding of the resurrection places our own death and the death of our loved ones and others in the proper perspective. There is much about the after-life that God has chosen not to reveal to us. But one thing is perfectly clear; all believers will live in eternity with Christ.

---

1. 1. Thess. 4.13-18; 2. John 11.25.

# Right Versus Wrong

Are there absolute standards parents may follow to teach their children right from wrong? The Bible tells us there are. "All Scripture is given by inspiration of God, and is profitable for doctrine, for reproof, for correction, for instruction in righteousness."[1] For thousands of years many have tried to discredit this claim, but the Bible has withstood the test of time and continues to be an even greater force in the world today.

God through His word presents principles for all aspects of living. He allows people freedom of choice. But this in no way changes His standards. "The fear (reverence) of the Lord is the beginning of wisdom, and the knowledge of the holy One in understanding."[2] Wisdom is God's point of view. God's word serves as an anchor in our constantly changing world. Though conditions and circumstances change, the principles remain the same. "Jesus Christ is the same yesterday, today and forever."[3]

Children need to have a clear understanding of the differences between right and wrong. Wrong comes naturally to children. Right must be learned. Parents need to spell it out for them. They are not capable of doing it on their own. There is no place for permissiveness in early childhood rearing. The idea that there are no absolutes, that truth is relative are popular but foolish concepts. Letting children make up their own minds about what's right and what's wrong is the source of much confusion.

The more specific, brief and certain parents can be about right versus wrong the less confused children will be about what is expected of them. "For if the trumpet makes an uncertain sound, who will prepare for the battle?"[4] There are no uncertain sounds in the Bible about right and wrong. It tells parents what's right and what isn't; what's responsible and acceptable behavior and what isn't. Morally, children need to hear crystal clear messages from adults regarding right versus wrong.

Children form impressions of right and wrong long before reaching school age. If they do not learn it from parents, they will learn it from television, friends, neighbors, on their own or some other unreliable source. "There is a way that seems right to a man, but its end is a way of death."[5] "Woe to those who call evil good, and good evil; who put darkness for light, and light for darkness; who put bitter for sweet, and sweet for bitter. Woe to those who are wise in their own eyes, and prudent in their own sight!"[6] God is the only unerroring authority to decide right from wrong.

Parents must have a definite set of moral values in place that their children can sense as they are growing up. Their personal lives should serve as a model of proper behavior. Learning about God's word and applying it to everyday living is the most important lesson parents can teach their children. " 'In that I command you today to love the Lord your God, to walk in His ways, and keep His commandments, His statutes, and His judgments, that you may live and multiply; and the lord your God will bless you . . . .' "[7] "Blessed is everyone who fears the Lord, who walks in His ways."[9] "Trust in the Lord with all your heart, and lean not on your own understanding; in all your ways acknowledge Him, and He shall direct your paths."[9]

Teaching children to live according to God's word will not be easy, especially when they see others doing wrong and getting away with it. The following passages speak directly to this matter. "Do not fret because of evildoers, nor be envious of the workers of iniquity. For they shall soon be cut down like the grass, and wither as the green herb. Rest in the Lord, and wait patiently for Him; do not fret because of him who prospers in his way. For evildoers shall be cut off; but those who wait on the Lord, they shall inherit the earth."[10] "For the Lord knows the way of the righteous, but the way of the ungodly shall perish."[11]

Children need to know that God is totally aware of everyone's actions, including those done in secret. "So then each of us shall give account of himself to God."[12] "God will render to each one according to his deeds."[13] "Wait on the Lord, and keep His way, and He shall exalt you to inherit the land; when the wicked are cut off, you shall see it."[14]

The final question in deciding right from wrong must always be: Does the action glorify or offend God? Parents must impress upon their children that they will reap what they sow.

---

1. 2 Tim. 3.16; 2. Prov. 9.10; 3. Heb. 13.8; 4. 1 Cor.14.8; 5. Prov. 16.25; 6. Is. 5.20, 21; 7. Deut. 30.16; 8. Ps. 128.1; 9. Prov. 3.5, 6; 10. Ps. 37.1, 2, 7, 9; 11. Ps. 1.6; 12. Rom. 14.12; 13. Rom. 2.6; 14. Ps. 37.34.

# Salvation

Jesus' death on the cross makes salvation possible to the believer. "Nor is there salvation in any other, for there is no other name under heaven given among men by which we must be saved."[1] "For whoever calls on the name of the Lord shall be saved."[2]

All who acknowledge their need for salvation, admit that they are by nature sinful, accept Christ as Lord and Savior and believe that God raised Him from the dead are assured of salvation. "Behold, now is the accepted time; behold, now is the day of salvation."[3] "For the wages of sin is death, but the gift of God is eternal life in Christ Jesus our Lord."[4] Jesus said, " 'I say to you, he who hears my word and believes in Him who sent Me has everlasting life, and shall not come into judgment, but has passed from death into life.' "[5] Salvation is to be forever in God's presence.

God's promise of salvation must be taught to children. "And this is the testimony: that God has given us eternal life, and this life is in His Son. He who has the Son has life; he who does not have the Son of God does not have life."[6] God holds parents responsible for preparing the ground, planting the seeds of salvation, and being faithful in their witness to their children. It's always appropriate for parents to pray God would draw their children into His kingdom.

Faith includes all that God requires for salvation. "For by grace you have been saved through faith, and that not of yourselves; it is the gift of God, not of works, lest anyone should boast."[7] " 'Behold, I stand at the door and knock. If anyone hears My voice and opens the door, I will come in to him and dine with him, and he with Me.' "[8] But as many as received

Him, to them He gave the right to become children of God, to those who believe in His name."[9] "For God so loved the world that He gave His only begotten Son, that whoever believes in Him should not perish but have everlasting life. For God did not send His Son into the world to condemn the world, but that the world through Him might be saved."[10]

The Bible teaches that salvation is the result of God's grace; no matter how good we are we could never earn salvation. As believers, God expects us to handle all of life's circumstances that come our way in a responsible manner, even though our salvation doesn't depend on it. It's a gift. "It is good that one should hope and wait quietly for the salvation of the Lord."[11] "Look to Me, and be saved ... there is no other."[12]

---

1. Acts 4.12; 2. Rom. 10.13; 3. 2 Cor. 6.2; 4. Rom. 6.23; 5. John 5.24; 6. 1 John 5.11, 12; 7. Eph. 2.8, 9; 8. Rev. 3.20; 9. John 1.12; 10. John 3.16, 17; 11. Lam. 3.26; 12. Is. 45.22.

# Self-Esteem

When we think well of ourselves, we are more inclined to respect others. Self-esteem is not self-centeredness. Nor is it a matter of seeing oneself as better than someone else. High self-esteem falls within the confines of God's word. It means seeing and accepting ourselves as God created us. Children must be informed that God loves them unconditionally. One can then say, with God's help "I can do all things through Christ who strengthens me."[1] The Bible goes on to say, "Let nothing be done through selfish ambition or conceit, but in lowliness of mind let each esteem others better than himself. Let each of you look out not only for his own interests but also for the interests of others."[2]

Children need self-esteem to give them the confidence to try new things without fear of failure. They also are less likely to be manipulated by those who would lead them down the wrong path. Children with low self-esteem feel inferior, unloved, unaccepted, unworthy, insecure and unhappy. Children with high self-esteem feel competent, loved, accepted, worthy, secure and happy.

Parents need to focus on as many positive aspects of children's personalities as possible. "Whatever things are true, whatever things are noble, whatever things are just, whatever things are pure, whatever things are lovely, whatever things are of good report, if there is any virtue and if there is anything praiseworthy — meditate on these things."[3] One of the most important responsibilities of parents is to help their children develop positive self-images.

Much of children's self-esteem comes from their parents. The more self-esteem parents display the greater the opportunity for children to develop healthy self-images. Children need to be encouraged to learn, do and succeed at as many things as possible. Parents need to assign responsibilities, establish good work habits and introduce new skills and hobbies in which children can succeed. Success reinforces self-esteem. It's very important that children do well in at least one thing.

Children are anxious to please parents. They want to be accepted and loved. When parents withhold their acceptance, love and praise or fail to acknowledge their efforts, children feel rejected, unworthy and unloved. They feel good about themselves when they please their parents. As they grow up this is transferred into pleasing God and learning that, "If God is for us, who can be against us?"[4] Children form their impression of God from their parents because parents are God in their eyes.

Parents need to remind their children that God will give them the help and strength they will need to do His will. Children who like themselves tend to do well. Those who don't won't. High self-esteem is basic to child development. When children have no self-esteem, they have no self-respect for themselves, for others and none for the world in which they live.

---

1. Phil. 4.13; 2. Phil. 2.3-4; 3. Phil. 4.8; 4. Rom. 8.31.

# Sin

Sin is a turning away from God. "Whoever commits sin also commits lawlessness, and sin is lawlessness."[1] It is any thought, word or action that is contrary to God's teachings. It forms a barrier that separates us from God; we want to live our way rather than His way. No one is without sin .... "There is none righteous (without sin) no, not one."[2] "If we say that we have no sin, we deceive ourselves, and the truth is not in us."[3] Only Jesus lived without sin.

Some people concern themselves more with certain sins than others. The "Seven Deadly Sins" in the writings of St. Thomas Aquinas are such an example:

1. PRIDE — an absorbing sense of one's own greatness often at the expense of others.
2. AVARICE — greed; covetousness; excessive desire of gaining and possessing wealth.
3. LUST — extreme desire for pleasure that is selfish and irresponsible.
4. ANGER — uncontrolled rage, hostility, revenge and resentment towards others.
5. GLUTTONY — excessive eating and drinking to the point of hurting the body.
6. ENVY — discontent over another's possessions or good fortune.
7. SLOTH — laziness; unwilling to work to the point of using others.

These sins are not listed as such in the Bible. God does not prioritize sin because all sin is deadly in one way or another. They are mentioned here briefly to illustrate a point and will be discussed in greater depth throughout this publication.

It's important that parents teach their children what sin is so they can cope with it when it comes up in their lives. They need to be encouraged to resist anything that may lead to sin because, "When desire is conceived, it gives birth to sin; and sin when it is fully grown, brings forth death."[4] "... Do you not know that a little leaven leavens the whole lump."[5] Sin is destructive. It harms the person committing the sin as well as the innocent.

Children often think they can break God's laws and not suffer the consequences, especially if nobody finds out. They, of course, only fool themselves. " 'For nothing is secret that will not be revealed, nor anything hidden that will not be known and come to light.' "[6] "... And be sure your sin will find you out."[7] Children need to understand when they disobey God's laws they reap the destructive consequences of that disobedience; when they obey God's laws they reap their blessings. "He who covers his sins will not prosper, but whoever confesses and forsakes them will have mercy.' "[8]

Children can be freed from the worst sin imaginable by genuinely confessing, asking God's forgiveness and repenting of that sin. "If we confess our sins, He is faithful and just to forgive us our sins and to cleanse us from all unrighteousness."[9] "As far as the east is from the west, so far has He removed our transgressions from us."[10] " 'Come now, and let us reason together,' " says the Lord, " 'though your sins are like scarlet, they shall be as white as snow; though they are red like crimson, they shall be as wool.' "[11] The slate is wiped clean allowing them to start each day new, refreshed and filled with hope. Sin keeps us away from God's presence but His presence keeps us away from sin.

---

1. 1. John 3.4; 2. Rom. 3.10; 3. 1 John 1.8; 4. James 1.15; 5. 1 Cor. 5.6; 6. Luke 8.17; 7. Num. 32.23; 8. Prov. 28.13; 9. 1 John 1.9; 10. Ps. 103.12; 11. Is. 1.18.

# Spiritual Birth

At some point all adults as well as children must, of their own free will, decide to accept Jesus as their personal Savior. Then spiritual birth will follow. Jesus says, " '... Unless one is born of water and the Spirit, he cannot enter the kingdom of God. That which is born of the flesh is flesh, and that which is born of the Spirit is spirit.' "[1] The flesh dies but the Spirit lives in eternity.

It's important for parents to know that most people who come to know Christ do so before they are old enough to leave home. Parents should do all they can to influence a spiritual birth but they can't do it all. Jesus says, " 'No one can come to Me unless the Father who sent Me draws him ....' "[2] The rebirth experience is a gradual unfolding process that continues throughout life, much like a baby grows into adulthood. Children are not born from above again because their parents are. They must experience this for themselves. Then God opens their eyes to a life with new meaning and purpose.

Children need to be taught they will never understand everything there is to know about God. " ... No one can find out the work that God does from beginning to end."[3] It is like each generation painting part of a painting; but no one sees the painting completed. This is the way God intended it to be, but by learning about God in His Holy Word and trusting in His promises, He will become such a power in their lives they will soon learn to do what is right in His sight.

Their way of living will change with their spiritual birth. "Therefore, if anyone is in Christ, he is a new creation; old things have passed away; behold, all things have become new."[4] First, they will trust more in God and less in themselves.

Second, they will seek God's guidance in all they think, say and do. Third, they will accept Christ as their personal Savior. God will become a never ending source of comfort, strength and joy in their lives. Spiritual birth is as much a miracle as physical birth. When Spiritual birth takes place Jesus supplies the energy and strength that leads to eternal life.

---

1. John 3.5, 6; 2. John 6.44; 3. Eccles. 3.11; 4. 2 Cor. 5.17.

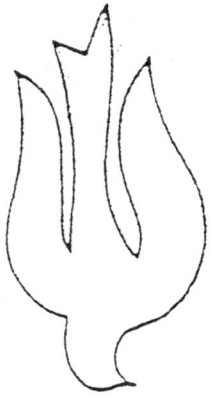

# Starting School

By the time children are old enough to start school, they have come a long way and learned a great deal. They have done much of it on their own with parents as their teachers. Parents can guide children's learning in practically every facet of life: fair play, respect, obedience, self-discipline, reading, writing, speaking, numbers, the alphabet, shapes, sizes, art, music, sports, science, gardening and good mental and physical health.

Before they begin school, parents should see to it that their children are familiar with and can perform certain tasks that will be expected of them by their teacher. In addition to looking after personal needs and getting along with other children, they will be expected to do such things as:

| | | |
|---|---|---|
| balance | know colors | go without a nap |
| skip | follow rules | complete activities |
| jump | correct mistakes | follow simple instructions |
| cut | play games | use of please and thank you |
| paste | feed themselves | ask and answer questions |
| color | clean up | catch and bounce a ball |

The smaller the gap between what parents teach their children and what the school expects, the easier the adjustment from home to school; and the more children will benefit from school.

Children will be expected to follow a schedule of school. Unless children have been required to live by some kind of schedule at home, they will start school with no real understanding of the concept of time. They need a certain amount of routine so they can feel organized: a time to eat, clean up, go to bed and a time to get up. They need experience in taking turns, getting dressed, learning good manners, being honest, treating others considerately and developing a sense of responsibility.

Parents must realize that children will differ in their ability to perform tasks at different age levels. Children tend to do their best even though at times it may not appear that way. Parents should resist the temptation of insisting their children perform for others. Parents should also avoid comparing their children with other children, especially brothers and sisters. It is best when children compete against themselves. By doing this they can see their progress and find satisfaction in it. Children must feel that they succeed or else they will stop trying.

Few parents realize how much their children have learned by age six. Gender-identity has been established; they have taken the turn that leads to being male or female. They have acquired two-thirds of their height. They will be one-third of the way toward being practically on their own. Some child experts say that by age six children learn over half of what they will ever know. Most of the seeds that determine behavior will have been planted. The kinds of fruit they will bear, during the next twelve years and the rest of their lives, will come from these seeds.

Parents who get down to business with their children when they start school are a little like the coach who meets with his players for the first time on the day of the game. Anyone who follows sports knows that to have good players a coach must do a lot of planning. He has played the game, studied it, read about it, enjoys almost everything about it. He prepares his players both physically and mentally, and winning more games than losing is considered a successful year. If children are going to be successful in school, they must be well coached during the pre-school years.

One of the areas that parents and educators need to look at very closely is the age at which children start school. Under the present system most children start in the September closest to their sixth birthdays, or nearest to their fifth birthdays for kindergarten. The assumption is that when children's birthdays fall within this range, they are all ready physically, mentally, and socially to start school. Nothing could be further from the truth.

Even if all children were born on the same day, they would vary greatly by age six. It's a little like a horse race. Even though all the horses start out together, they become quite spread out by the end of the race.

Children don't walk, talk, toilet train, or have the same interests at the same time; and it is unlikely that they would all be ready to read, write, do math, and cope socially at the same time.

There could be as much as one year age difference among children in the same classroom. Attendance laws vary from state to state. For example, in some states parents may enroll their children in September as long as they turn six by January 31. Those children who turn six January 31 would be the youngest in their class. Children born on February 1 and after would have to wait until the following September to start. There could be as much as a one-year difference between the two extreme age groups. They could be sitting next to each other and most teachers would expect them to learn the same material at about the same time and behave as first graders "SHOULD."

This is not to say that there is not a definite relationship between age and maturity but there are many exceptions. A six-year-old may look like most six-year-olds physically, but his mental development may be closer to that of a five-year-old at that point in his life and of course the opposite may be true. Most children young for their age struggle in school and end up with a poor self-image. The older, more mature children may be bored at times but they are successful and usually feel pretty good about themselves.

Many school districts are aware of the problems that result from early enrollment and have adopted cut-off dates that are less liberal than state attendance laws. For example, children must be five years old by September to enroll in kindergarten. This is the school's way of keeping younger children out.

They can insist on this cut-off date for kindergarten, but not first grade, because first grade is compulsory and kindergarten isn't.

Parents try to get around this by having children tested by psychologists who usually tell them what they want to hear: that their children have the intelligence and to enroll them in school. Of course they have the intelligence! They had it at birth. Intelligence is usually not the problem. The problem is that they just haven't lived as long as most children in the class. Even though they may appear equal or superior to other children in the neighborhood, the fact remains they haven't lived as long. After a short period of time in school, the younger children will start to lag behind. The gap between them will become greater just as the gap between horses in a race will widen. The longer they run the more spread out they become. The younger children become the 50 to 1 odds of finishing first.

When this age group isn't permitted to enroll in kindergarten, parents often send their children to nursery school and enroll them in first grade when the state attendance law permits. This doesn't solve the problem. Nursery school and kindergarten cannot speed up maturity, just as dressing teenagers in "grown up" clothes can't make them adults.

In addition to these children being younger, it's quite possible that they may be a year or more less mature because of their make up. Also, girls, generally, are more mature physically and mentally from birth through the teenage years by as much as a year or more. When all these factors are taken into consideration — children who are younger by one year because of their birthdate, children who are less mature because they develop slower, and the maturity difference between boys and girls — we are talking about a possible three-year age difference.

Allowing children to start school before they are ready often leads to a continuous struggle of playing "catch up." In many instances, it means the difference between liking or hating school. Three out of four younger boys and one out of four younger girls encounter serious difficulties at school. The younger boys and girls who do succeed are usually very intelligent and come from above average homes. Even in these cases, one can't help wondering whether they would not have done even better with children their own age.

Age is not a perfect method to determine when children start school; but it's unlikely to change in the near future. Therefore, parents must rely on their own judgment along with guidance from their school systems. My recommendation is that children who turn six in June or later of that year (five for kindergarten) should not enroll in first grade that September, but rather wait until the following September. These children will be seven (six for kindergarten) when they start school. This means that all first graders will be seven years old by the end of the school year. By keeping summer birthday children out of school until the following year will allow the children to reach age eighteen before high school graduation rather than after.

For these younger children already having trouble or really hating school, it's not too late to do something about their lack of success. If this is happening early in their schooling, chances are the situation will not get better as many teachers and principals promise and parents hope. It probably will get worse. If immaturity is the problem, the gap will widen more each year and achievement will continue to drop off. Coping socially becomes more difficult. When children can't keep up, they'll be teased about it. And most of all, their lack of success will result in a poor self-image. If this is still happening through third grade (assuming there are not learning disabilities), retention is worth the risk. This isn't nearly as cruel or traumatic as most parents think. Children adjust quickly. It is much more cruel to do nothing and allow children to go through the remaining years of school trying to "catch up."

By eighth grade (thirteen years old) the situation may become impossible for children, parents and teachers. These children, even though they have the ability, fail to apply themselves. Poor achievement becomes a constant source of bickering and frustration in school and in the home. Even at this late stage, if it's a maturity problem, retention can still be in the best interest of the child.

Also, parents need to consider the long range social implications of starting school a little younger than most other children. Grade level dictates what will be expected of children. Children may be forced into social situations before they are ready. If a dance is scheduled for seventh graders, the younger children will want to go even though they are closer to sixth grade age. When the junior prom rolls around, they will be sophomore age. There's already too much emphasis in our society for youngsters to grow up before their time; starting school at a younger age adds to this. If they go out for a sport, they have to compete against older classmates. If they have done less than their best through school, they may not do as well on college boards or scholarship tests.

At graduation they will not turn eighteen until later that summer, limiting their job opportunities. If they go on their own or off to college, they do so with a little less experience and younger than most of their peers. When in doubt, starting later is better than starting earlier.

# Stewardship

A steward is one who manages what belongs to others. Christians know that God is the maker of all; therefore all belongs to Him. "The earth is the Lord's and all its fullness, the world and those who dwell therein."[1] That makes us all stewards whose job it is to manage all of what God has created and given to us. We must all give account of our stewardship.

Giving doesn't come easily, especially to children. Human nature leans much more toward getting. It's only when we surrender ourselves to God that we begin to understand Jesus' word when He said, " 'It is more blessed to give than to receive.' "[2] When the habit of giving is cultivated in children, they will soon discover that the more generous and faithful they are in their giving the more devoted they will become to Christ.

Tithing is one of God's specific giving laws. It means returning one-tenth of one's income to God to promote His Kingdom. Why is it so important parents instill the proper attitude about resources given to their children? The following Bible passages speak to this question. "Will a man rob God? Yet you have robbed Me! But you say, 'In what way have we robbed You?' In tithes and offerings."[3] "Honor the Lord with your possessions, and with the first fruits of all your increases."[4] "There is one who scatters, yet increases more; and there is one who withholds more than is right, but it leads to poverty. The generous soul will be made rich, and he who waters will also be watered himself."[5]

Rich and poor, old and young, every believer should give. "On the first day of the week let each of you lay something aside, storing up as he may prosper ...."[6] "So let each one of us give as he purposes (intends) in his heart, not grudgingly or of necessity; for God loves a cheerful giver.' "[7]

There are many ways to give. Parents need to teach their children that tithing is just one of them. Jesus said, " 'Woe to you, scribes and Pharisees, hypocrites! For you pay tithe of mint and anise and cumin, and have neglected the weightier matters of the law: justice and mercy and faith. These you ought to have done, without leaving the others undone.' "[8]

" '. . . I say to you, inasmuch as you did it to one of the least of these My brethren, you did it to Me.' "[9] In addition to money children should be encouraged to give of their time, talents and possessions or any of the many other gifts they may have to offer.

Giving, no matter what it may be, is like seed: the more sown the greater the harvest. ". . . He who sows sparingly will also reap sparingly, and he who sows bountifully will also reap bountifully."[10]

Giving never diminishes us. In fact the opposite is true. The more we give the more we have to give and the more we will be blessed. We know from other areas of life that the more we put in to something the more we get out. People are less inclined to believe this about giving but that doesn't make it less true. Parents need to remind their children that their giving not only helps others, it benefits them as well. More importantly, giving glorifies God! Those who honor God with their gifts are in return blessed.

---

1. Ps. 24.1; 2. Acts 20.35; 3. Mal. 3.8; 4. Prov. 3.9; 5. Prov. 11.24, 25; 6. 1 Cor. 16.2; 7. 2 Cor. 9.7; 8. Matt. 23.23; 9. Matt. 25.40; 10. 2 Cor. 9.6.

# Talent

We have all been born with certain God-given talents, abilities and aptitudes. Everyone is different. " ...Each one has his own gift from God, one in this manner and another in that."[1] "Having then gifts differing according to the grace that is given to us, let us use them ...."[2] "Do not neglect the gift that is in you ...."[3] God expects each person to grow, develop and use the talents, abilities and aptitudes He has given them.

Children can easily be made to feel inadequate if denied the Biblical point of view regarding talent. The Bible teaches that every human being has an important place in God's Kingdom. Children differ physically, mentally and emotionally. One of the greatest gifts parents can give their children is to help them identify their unique talents. Nurturing and motivating them in those talents not only pleases them, it pleases God.

God's expectations never exceed a child's gifts and talents. Children are responsible for only what God has endowed them. It's very comforting for children, and adults also, to know that they don't have to be like everybody else.

God in His divine wisdom and love did not make us all alike. He made some more talented than others as illustrated in the parable of the talents. "And to one He gave five talents, to another two, and to another one, to each according to his own ability ...."[4] The one who had received five talents traded with them and made another five talents. He who had received two gained two more also. He who had received one went and dug in the ground and hid his lord's money. The two servants who doubled their five and two talents were praised equally by their master. The one who had hid and returned his one talent was condemned by his master and even that was taken from him. " 'For to everyone who has, more will be given, and he will have abundance; but from him who does not have, even what he has will be taken away.' "[5] Parents must see to it that their children don't bury or hide their talents, abilities and gifts.

Parents should encourage their children to thank God and praise Him for their many blessings, their time, talents, abilities and tangible goods. Ask His guidance in using them to advance His Kingdom and to glorify His name to the best of their ability.

---

1. 1 Cor. 7.7; 2. Rom. 12.6; 3. 1 Tim. 4.14; 4. Matt. 25.15; 5. Matt. 25.29.

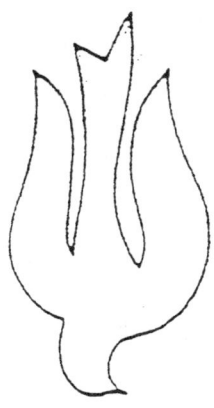

# Teaching

Parents are the first and most important teachers their children will ever have. Informal learning takes place in the home through experience and example while school systems take care of formal education. Whatever children learn in the home, right or wrong, tends to remain with them throughout life. They will insist something they learned from their parents is right even when it's wrong. Teachers are often at a loss to help children overcome undesirable habits and incorrect information acquired during childhood.

Contrary to what many people think the amount of formal education parents have is not the major factor in how children do in school and life. Parents who care about their children and practice Biblical child-rearing principles are the most effective.

Babies learn more during the first year of life than at any other time. They are capable of learning much more than most parents realize. Successful parents stimulate learning in their children during the pre-school years by doing the following:

1. Answer their children's questions with patience and good humor.
2. Take advantage of their questions as a guide to further learning.
3. Help them learn how to get along with other children and have their friends over.
4. Don't compare them with brothers, sisters or companions, but rather have them compete against themselves. "But let each one examine his own work, and then he will have rejoicing in himself alone, and not in another."[1]

116

5. Unconditionally love their children.
6. Set reasonable standards of behavior and see that they're met.
7. Provide early opportunities for responsibility and decision-making appropriate to their age level.
8. Praise their accomplishments — praise publicly and discipline privately.
9. Help them find worthwhile reading materials and be very selective in their television viewing.
10. Provide hobby materials, work areas and display their work.
11. Share some of their own hobbies and interests.
12. Take them on trips.
13. Hug, kiss, sing, talk, play and laugh with them.
14. Give children increasing independence as their ability to handle responsibility increases.
15. Resist the temptation to exploit and show their children off.
16. Teach their children that they are no less or no more important than anybody else.
17. Provide a loving environment so children can thrive physically, emotionally and Spiritually. Parent, "Do not provoke your children to wrath, but bring them up in the training and admonition of the Lord."[2]
18. Set an example for the kind of attitude and behavior they expect of their children. What parents say will influence their children only if it's supported by their actions. Boys tend to imitate their fathers and girls their mother. This is very healthy when parents are good role models.

Teaching moral principles is an on-going process. Parents have to be with their children especially during the pre-school years. In children's eyes their parents are God. So before they can teach their children about God, they must make sure they are representing Him accurately.

---

1. Gal. 6.4; 2. Eph. 6.4.

117

# Television

Television is one of the greatest inventions of all time. Since the 1950s it has affected peoples' lives more than any other technological development. For the first time in history something other than parents has become the main provider of information, values and entertainment for children. TV has changed how the family functions, how people think, what they buy, how they dress, and what they do during their free time.

Surveys tell us that average pre-school age children, ages 2 to 5, spend a third or more of their total waking hours watching TV. Most children will spend more time watching TV than any other single activity during the first 18 years of their lives except sleep.

Television can be a great blessing. At its best it can inform, expand and enrich the lives of adults and children. But it can also be a curse. It can rob adults and children of their moral and spiritual values and cripple their mental, emotional and physical development. The wrong use of television can:

1. cause confusion between right and wrong.
2. retard social development.
3. make learning in school more difficult.
4. shorten attention span.
5. reduce attentiveness.
6. discourage self discipline.
7. harm parent-child relationship.
8. interfere with meal time.
9. increase boredom.
10. promote spectatorship rather than participationship.

11. rob time from reading, writing, conversing, playing, exercising and imagining.
12. mislead children into believing difficult problems can be easily solved in a short period of time.

Parents are responsible for preventing television from ruling their family. They should not assume that TV is always acceptable entertainment. In fact, the opposite is true. TV programming is saturated with violence, sex, distorted role models, trivia and immorality. In addition to all of the above and more, TV viewing is extremely passive. Children put little into it; therefore, they get little value out of it. Plus, they've wasted valuable time that could be put to better use.

Parents should be very selective about which programs they allow their children to view, including the nightly ''news'' programs. The emphasis on violence, and dramatic footage can be very disturbing and destructive. The mass media is a major force in forming our attitudes of right and wrong. Most television writers and producers are convinced that focus on the ''forbidden fruit'' will increase the demand for their product because they think that's what the viewing public wants. As a result broadcasting guidelines are pushed to the limit in downgrading language, moral values, good taste, speech, dress, manners, respect, kindness, and concern for others.

Often the programs are so captivating that even Christians fail to change channels or turn off the TV. The Bible says, ''Do not be conformed to this world, but be transformed by the renewing of your mind, that you may prove what is that good and acceptable and perfect will of God.''[1] God's word should serve as the final authority on what we should accept or reject from the broadcasting industry.

According to the American Academy of Pediatrics, children should be limited to watching no more than two hours of TV a day. It helps to decide ahead of time which programs to watch. Having only one TV in the home will help to achieve this goal.

The time gained can then be spent on more constructive activities. They could include such things as reading, using the library, listening to good radio programming, playing games, conversing with friends and family members, taking trips, learning to get along with others and many other activities where children are actively involved gaining life-lasting skills and benefits.

---

1. Rom. 12.2.

# Temptation

Temptation is anything that lures or entices us to act outside of God's will. It's not a sin to be tempted but it is sinful to yield to it. "Let no one say when he is tempted, 'I am tempted of God'; for God cannot be tempted by evil, nor does He Himself tempt anyone. But each one is tempted when he is drawn away by his own desires and enticed. Then when desire has conceived it gives birth to sin; and sin, when it is full-grown, brings forth death."[1]

When children find themselves tempted to act outside God's will, parents should encourage them to ask: What would happen if I yielded? Would it be worth the consequences? They should be honest in thinking through the outcome. Ask God for strength to resist temptation. " 'Watch and pray, lest you enter into temptation. The spirit indeed is willing, but the flesh is weak.' "[2]

"No temptation has overtaken you except such as in common to man; but God is faithful, who will not allow you to be tempted beyond what you are able, but with the temptation will also make the way of escape, that you may be able to bear it."[3] "Blessed is the man who endures temptation; for when he has been approved, he will receive the crown of life which the Lord has promised to those who love Him."[4] By trusting in what God says is right and doing what God would have them do, children can be assured that God's grace will be there to help them resist temptation where and when they need it.

---

1. James 1.13-15; 2. Matt. 26.41; 3. 1 Cor. 10.13; 4. James 1.12.

# The Ten Commandments

The Ten Commandments are the foundation of our morality: what is right and just in human conduct. They have provided wisdom through the centuries and remain relevant today. "For this is the love of God that we keep His commandments. And His commandments are not burdensome."[1]

The commandments can be divided into two groups. The first four tell us how to love God. The remaining six tell us how to love our neighbors. The brief discussion of each commandment is to help the reader relate it to everyday life. "... Fear (respect) God and keep His commandments, for this is man's all (purpose)."[2] "And God spoke all these words, saying:"[3]

---

1. 1 John 5.3; 2. Eccles. 12.13; 3. Ex. 20.1-17.

# First Commandment

"YOU SHALL HAVE NO OTHER GODS BE-FORE ME" .... Jesus referred to the first commandment as the greatest commandment of all. " '... You shall love the Lord your God with all your heart, and with all your soul, and with all your mind.' "[1] In addition to it being the most important, it also is the most challenging to obey.

The needs and wants of everyday living can often overwhelm us with demands on our time and energy. These can interfere with keeping God first. Work, family, educational pursuits and leisure time activities can all become substitute gods in our lives. They are sinful when given higher priority than God: God first, people second and things third.

---

1. Matt. 22.37.

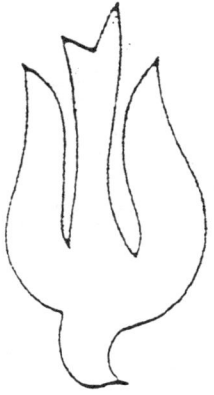

# Second Commandment

"YOU SHALL NOT MAKE FOR YOURSELF A CARVED IMAGE" ... Worshipping idols is idolatry. The second commandment forbids making graven images of a person, place or thing and using it as an object of worship. God is not material. " 'God is Spirit, and those who worship Him must worship in spirit and truth.' "[1]

The commandment goes on to say that the sins of the parents will pass on to the next generation. While each of us is responsible for what he or she does or does not do, we are also affected by the actions of those around us; and what we do seldom affects only us. The consequences are clear. Our children and their children and their children's children may be either blessed or cursed by how we conduct ourselves as parents.

---

1. John 4.24.

## Third Commandment

"YOU SHALL NOT TAKE THE NAME OF THE LORD YOUR GOD IN VAIN" . . . The third commandment reminds us of our proper respect of God. When we take the Lord's name in vain, it's always done in anger and when things have not gone our way. Aware of it or not, it shows preoccupation with self and total disrespect for God. Instead of accepting responsibility for our own actions, we blame God, the one who can best help us if we will seek His wisdom.

The Bible teaches that God is the creator and ruler of the universe. The Psalmist reminds us of God's glory and man's honor. "O Lord, our Lord, how excellent is Your name in all the earth, who have set Your glory above the heavens! When I consider Your heavens, the work of Your fingers, the moon and the stars, which You have ordained, what is man that You are mindful of him, and the son of man that You visit him? For You have made him a little lower than the angels, and You have crowned him with glory and honor. You have made him to have dominion over the works of Your hands; You have put all things under his feet."[1] This is what people condemn when they take the Lord's name in vain.

---

1. Ps. 8.1, 3-6.

# Fourth Commandment

"REMEMBER THE SABBATH DAY, TO KEEP IT HOLY" . . . The fourth commandment tells us that the Lord blessed the Sabbath day and hallowed it. " 'And God rested on the seventh day from all His works.' "[1] And this is the message to us. The purpose of the Sabbath is for rest, worship and to renew our spirit. It was ordained at creation, honored throughout the Old and New Testament titles and is relevant today as it was then. Jesus said, " '. . . The Sabbath was made for man, not man for the Sabbath.' "[2] This special day of the week is intended by God to be a blessing for all.

Many think this commandment shouldn't be taken as seriously as the other nine, which explains why it is disobeyed so often. People try to explain it away by saying there's too much to do; it ruins the weekend; it interferes with work. The truth of the matter is the more busy people allow themselves to become the greater the need to honor the Sabbath. This places work in the proper perspective with our spiritual needs. After all, what are we working for?

Choosing to honor the Sabbath sets a good example for children. This will make sense to them. It will also help them understand the importance of obeying the other commandments. Also, it will help them be more aware of God's place in our lives and how important it is to obey Him. Children need to be taught that when they disobey this commandment, they jeopardize their mental, physical and spiritual health.

---

1. Heb. 4.4; 2. Mark 2.27.

# Fifth Commandment

 "HONOR YOUR FATHER AND MOTHER" ...
The fifth commandment speaks to children; but parents have
a lot to do with how they carry it out. Young children view
their parents as God. How parents handle this assigned responsibility will greatly influence how their children come to view
first them and then God.

Parents need to live lives worthy of their children's honor
and respect. They also have to teach their children to obey,
respect and honor them. How else will they know? The Bible
tells fathers and mothers to follow certain guidelines in training their children. For example, "... Do not provoke your
children to wrath, but bring them up in the training and admonition of the Lord."[1] It's another way of saying: "Parents
have to earn their children's respect."

---

1. Eph. 6.4.

## Sixth Commandment

"YOU SHALL NOT MURDER" ... God creates life and values it. No one has the right to destroy it. There is little comfort in the fact that the sixth commandment is broken the least.

Most of us wouldn't even think of pulling the trigger to snuff out a life, yet many are guilty of another kind of murder. Jesus said, " 'You have heard that it was said to those of old, 'you shall not murder, and whoever murders will be in danger of the judgment.' But I say to you that whoever is angry with his brother without a cause shall be in danger of the judgment ....' "[1] When we harbor hate and anger, we are guilty by association of murdering the spirit. "Whoever hates his brother is a murderer, and you know that no murderer has eternal life abiding in him."[2]

Thoughtless and selfish acts can kill. They can kill hope for eternity, reputation, happiness, peace, joy and much more. God loves every human being He creates. So when we hurt or destroy any one of His children, we sin against the Creator .... "I say to you, 'inasmuch as you did it to one of the least of these My brethren, you did it to Me.' "[3]

---

1. Matt. 5.21, 22; 2. 1 John 3.15; 3. Matt. 25.40.

128

# Seventh Commandment

"YOU SHALL NOT COMMIT ADULTERY" . . . The seventh commandment, like the fifth, is directed at nurturing relationships in the home and family. Marriage, as ordained by God, is a holy institution. Its purpose includes companionship, sexual enjoyment, children and character development. The Bible teaches that sexual intercourse is to take place within the marriage relationships.

Infidelity is offensive to husbands, wives, children, society and God. It is the source of many negative consequences such as suspicion, anxiety, pain, anger, sexual diseases, family breakdowns and divorce. "Whoever commits adultery with a woman lacks understanding; He who does so destroys his own soul."[1] Jesus elaborates on this commandment as He did in the sixth, " 'You have heard that it was said to those of old, 'you shall not commit adultery.' But I say to you that whoever looks at a woman to lust for her has already committed adultery with her in his heart."[2] The implication being that thoughts precede actions. There are many factors besides fidelity that make up a good marriage. But, the fact that one of only ten commandments deals specifically with this topic gives it a very high priority.

---

1. Prov. 6.32; 2. Matt. 5.27, 28.

# Eighth Commandment

"YOU SHALL NOT STEAL" ... There's no question about the meaning of this commandment. Most agree with it and civil laws enforce it. It looks out for everyone's interest. And yet, it is one of the most violated commandments. Most would think twice about stealing something if they knew they might get caught. But it's an entirely different story if they think they can get away with it. This kind of thinking is bad enough in children but inexcusable in adults.

Those who decide to steal fail to understand that as the guilty party they will pay in the long run, after enjoying their temporary gain. "So each of us shall give account of himself to God."[1] Stealing is wrong and therefore can not turn out right. This point needs to be stressed to children.

Many children learn to steal on their own. It seems that they don't need any instructions. Parents need to do everything possible to be a good example for their children to follow. They should not allow children to take even little things that don't belong to them; even if there's no chance of anyone finding out. God knows. Stress the fact that, "... There is nothing covered that will not be revealed, and hidden that will not be known."[2] Children need to be taught that not getting caught doesn't make it right. If they swallow poison when nobody is looking, they still will die!

---

1. Rom. 14.12; 2. Matt. 10.26.

# Ninth Commandment

"YOU SHALL NOT BEAR FALSE WITNESS AGAINST YOUR NEIGHBOR" ... The ninth commandment reminds us of God's concern for His children and it should be ours as well. " '... You shall love your neighbor as yourself.' "[1] Obviously, many people choose to do otherwise.

Why would anyone purposely misrepresent their neighbor? The possibilities are endless: anger, envy, jealousy, revenge, selfishness, hate, rejection, personal gain, avoid responsibility, character assassination and many more. The Bible teaches that none of those constitute justifiable cause. "Do not be a witness against your neighbor without cause, for would you deceive with your lips?"[2] "A false witness will not go unpunished, and he who speaks lies will not escape."[3] No where are we told that we can right a wrong with another wrong.

Parents must teach their children that lying is a sin. All forms of deception, including "little white lies," are all condemned in God's word. "Let no corrupt word proceed out of your mouth, but what is good for necessary edification (building others up), that it may impart grace to the hearers."[4] Children who lie about little things grow up to lie about big things. " 'He who is faithful in what is least is faithful also in much; and he who is unjust in what is least is unjust also in much.' "[5] The more children lie the better they become at it. It doesn't take long for them to be branded liars, a reputation that may stick a lifetime. People are only as good as their word!

---

1. James 2.8; 2. Prov. 24.28; 3. Prov. 19.5; 4. Eph. 4.29; 5. Luke 16.10.

131

# Tenth Commandment

"YOU SHALL NOT COVET" ... The tenth commandment tells us not to covet anything that belongs to another. When we desire something to the point of envy, we have gone too far. We have broken the commandment. " 'Take heed and beware of covetousness, for one's life does not consist in the abundance of the things he possesses.' "[1] "Let your conduct be without covetousness; be content with such things as you have. For He Himself has said, 'I will never leave you nor forsake you.' "[2]

We can become so preoccupied with what we don't have that we fail to appreciate what we do have. It's like people sitting around starving themselves because they want to eat only the food that others have rather than eat their own. This commandment says, "eat what you have." Don't go hungry and then complain about it.[1]

God cares about our physical well-being as well as our spiritual health. He says to us, " 'But seek first the kingdom of God and His righteousness, and all these things shall be added to you.' "[3] When we focus on what we don't have much of life ends up being lived in the unfulfilled future, denying us the opportunity of making the most of the present. Covetousness cuts us off from God's strength, peace, joy and many more of His other blessings.

---

1. Luke 12.15; 2. Heb. 13.5; 3. Matt. 6.33.

# Time

Time is something in very limited supply. Why not invest it in our children? When parents spend time with their children, they pay them the highest compliment they will ever receive. The Bible cautions us about not taking time for granted. "Whereas you do not know what will happen tomorrow. For what is your life? It is even a vapor that appears for a little time and then vanishes away."[1]

Using time wisely means establishing priorities. Children should be first on your list. They can't wait. You should be involved with every facet of their lives. Children can't survive physically or emotionally when left on their own. They need loving care and guidance especially during the pre-school years. This is when they can best absorb the character-building values they will need the rest of their lives. "Train up a child in the way he should go, and when he is old he will not depart from it."[2] If these values are not learned at an early age they may never be learned. The Bible tells us: "To everything there is a season, a time for every purpose under heaven. A time to be born, and a time to die; a time to plant, and a time to pluck what is planted."[3]

Time between parents and children is needed to focus on such things as:

1. Enjoying them for what they are.
2. Building up their self-esteem.
3. Helping them set small and large goals.
4. Making home a happy place to be.
5. Teaching them to accept the bad along with the good.
6. Helping them to be good at as many things as possible.
7. Encouraging them to become as independent as possible.

8. Helping them develop realistic self-concepts.
9. Showing them how to do things.
10. Reading to them.
11. Loving, talking, singing, touching and playing.
12. Allowing them to help.
13. Getting to know each other.
14. Learning about God and praying together.
15. Encouraging them to make the most of their God given gifts.
16. Acknowledging differences in children by not comparing them.

Time spent with children helps parents learn about their personalities, opinions, and talents. What a joy to discover the individual God created! Time with your children is a priceless gift from God. Wasting this time dishonors Him.

------

1. James 4.14; 2. Prov. 22.6; 3. Eccles. 3.1, 2.

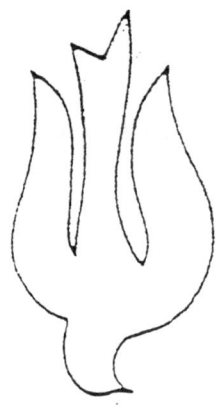

# Truth

Truthfulness is a character trait that needs to be instilled very early in children. They will face many opportunities when they will be tempted to avoid or turn from the truth because of the cost involved. It's important they decide in advance how they will react when such occasions arise. They may find it hard to do at first but such experiences help them stand for what is right when there's pressure from their peers to compromise their integrity. "Stand therefore, having girded your waist with truth, having put on the breastplate of righteousness."[1] Jesus was never influenced by what people might think when He stated His truths.

Parents, by example, can best teach their children the principles of truthfulness. It is at this junction in their young lives that they decide which fork in the road they will take. The road of God's truth or the road of self-truth. "Therefore putting away lying, 'let each one of you speak truth with his neighbor,' for we are members of one another."[2] "Buy the truth, and do not sell it, also wisdom and instruction and understanding."[3] " . . . God our savior desires all men to be saved and to come to the knowledge of the truth."[4] This acquired truth allows God to be in charge of our lives.

One of God's most exciting promises is found in John's Gospel where Jesus said, " '. . . If you abide in My word, you are My disciples indeed. And you shall know the truth and the truth shall make you free.' "[5] Freedom from the weaknesses of human nature. Freedom from thoughts, words and actions that hurt and destroy self and others. Freedom from earthly sin that leads to eternal death. This acquired freedom allows God to direct our lives so we can reap His many blessings.

---

1. Eph. 6.14; 2. Eph. 4.25; 3. Prov. 23.23; 4. 1 Tim. 2.4; 5. John 8.31, 32.

# Values

There is a growing trend in the thinking that anything goes. There is no right or wrong. It's happening in many homes, schools, government and society in general: devotion to God, honesty, tolerance, respect and ethical behavior are just a few of the traditional values eroding around us. A growing number of people are interested only in fulfilling their own desires. "There is a way that seems right to a man, but its end is the way of death."[1]

Are there true basic values that will serve everyone under all circumstances and at all times? Christianity teaches that there are. "Trust in the Lord with all your heart, and lean not on your own understanding. In all your ways acknowledge him, and He shall direct your path."[2] "Whatever things are true, whatever things are noble, whatever things are just, whatever things are pure, whatever things are lovely, whatever things are of good report, if there is any virtue and if there is anything praise worthy — meditate on these things."[3] The ultimate test of whether values are true or false is whether or not they are acceptable to God. " . . . It is not in man who walks to direct his own steps."[4]

Finally, children learn their values from parents. Parents' values become their children's values. They unconsciously absorb them from birth on. The values children adopt before they go to school will be a major factor in how they will do in school and life. If they have been instilled with such basic values as respect for authority, self-discipline and obedience, they will learn and benefit from what school has to offer.

Children need to know that the Bible is the one place they can go for dependable help when trying to decide right from wrong. And that this applies to all people, all the time and under all circumstances. "All Scripture is given by inspiration of God, and is profitable for doctrine, for reproof, for correction, for instruction in righteousness."[5]

---

1. Prov. 14.12; 2. Prov. 3.5, 6; 3. Phil. 4.8; 4. Jer. 10.23; 5. 2 Tim. 3.16.

# Waste

Waste has become one of the most critical issues in today's society. But waste does more than fill up our trash cans. It is the useless expenditure of time, money, effort, talent and other valuable resources. It's what is squandered after our needs are met. It's carelessness, it's thoughtlessness, it's irresponsible behavior. "But whoever has this world's goods, and sees his brother in need, and shuts up his heart from him, how does the love of God abide in him?"[1]

The Bible is very clear about not wasting. For example, when Jesus fed the five thousand and they were filled, He said to His disciples, " 'Gather up the fragments that remain, so that nothing is lost (wasted).' "[2] Use what you need but don't deny others through waste.

Children learn wasteful or conserving habits from their parents' example. For example, energy experts say that we waste as much energy as we really need because lights, appliances and water are not turned off. There are many ways of preventing waste. As minor as they may seem, it can really add up when millions of people pull together. Waste is sinful because others suffer as a result of it. Children need to be taught to think about the welfare of others and not just their own.

---

1. 1 John 3.17; 2. John 6.12.

# Work

One of the goals of parenthood is to make work meaningful to children. For Christians, all work that glorifies God is honorable. ". . . Whatever you do, do it to the glory of God."[1] With God, what we do isn't nearly as important as how we do it. Why we do it. And for what reason. "In all your ways acknowledge Him, and He shall direct your paths."[2] Children need to be taught that we all need and depend on other people. This helps them appreciate what others do.

It's very important children learn to work as soon as possible. If they don't learn early they may never learn. Good work habits will help them with their school work because school is work. Work teaches responsibility, a sense of accomplishment, self-satisfaction and preparation for life. "When you eat the labor of your hands, you shall be happy, and it shall be well with you."[3]

Children will spend about half of their waking hours in school related matters. This will be their work. In most cases this will be their main job. It's not unlike most of the work that parents do. Not all of it will be fun and games. They need to be encouraged to view their schooling as something important and necessary for preparation of life. "And whatever you do, do it heartily, as to the Lord and not to men, Knowing that from the Lord you will receive the reward of the inheritance; for you serve the Lord Christ."[4] When children have a sense of God's presence in their lives, their attitude about work could well become an adventure in love.

Preparing children for the work force begins early in life. Although children are primarily interested in earning spending money, most parents realize the values acquired in work-related activities such as responsibility, persistence, punctuality, courtesy, dependability and honesty are the important things children will gain. It's a known fact that children are more appreciative when they work for what they get and they spend money more wisely when they have earned it. For these reasons alone parents should go out of their way to find jobs for even those too young to hold part-time jobs: house work, yard work, working for relatives and neighbors and the elderly. Not only is this good training for children and parents, others stand to benefit as well. Parents should:

1. Assign tasks that are appropriate to age and development.
2. Work along with children.
3. Don't expect perfection.
4. Make work appear pleasant and positive.
5. Children should not expect pay for doing routine chores.
6. Encourage and praise generously.
7. Require that they do their best.
8. Follow through with assigned tasks even if it's more trouble than doing it yourself. It will pay off later.

Have children begin with such tasks as tidying up, care of personal possessions, cleaning up their own mess, putting away toys and clothes, dressing themselves, setting the table and many other tasks around the house.

The sooner parents expect responsible behavior from their children the sooner they will come through. Parents must help their children understand that great accomplishments in life require great effort and hard work. Nothing really worthwhile comes easily but the rewards await them. There's no other activity in life that provides more satisfaction to more people during a lifetime than work that is acceptable in God's sight and glorifies His name.

---

1. 1 Cor. 10.31; 2. Prov. 3.6; 3. Ps. 128.2; 4. Col. 3.23, 24.

# Worldliness

Worldliness is that world system of unbelievers driven by greed, ambition and selfishness for gain at all cost. It relates to materialism, wealth, possessions, power and status as opposed to allegiance to a caring, loving, faithful and forgiving God. "For the love of money (and all it can do) is a root of all kinds of evil."[1] Many people who profess to believe in God worship worldly things rather than God. Worldliness, then, are those things contrary to God's will.

One of the most notable accounts of a worldly person is recorded in the book of Ecclesiastes. Solomon tells us he had outdone everyone. He had acquired everything a man could want: unsurpassed wisdom, pleasure beyond compare, unequalled fortune in gold and silver, great works, houses, vineyards, gardens, great herds and flocks, male and female singers, musicians, wines, food, 700 wives, 300 concubines and every other thing imaginable to satisfy his every pleasure. He acquired every material possession. He accomplished everything he wanted to accomplish. And did not withhold from any pleasure.

Solomon discovered that everything he thought he wanted wasn't enough. He concluded that " ... Indeed all was vanity and grasping for wind ...."[2] Solomon wants us to know that nothing under the sun really satisfies. God is the source of lasting meaning and satisfaction. Even when people are successful in acquiring possession, disappointment awaits them.

The Scripture has much to say about worldliness. Following is a selection of those passages. Jesus said we are to be mindful of the things of God not of the world. " 'For what will it profit a man if he gains the whole world and loses his soul? . . .' " [3] "Do you not know that friendship with the world is enmity with God? Whoever therefore wants to be a friend of the world makes himself an enemy of God." [4] "Do not love the world or the things in the world. If anyone loves the world, the love of the Father is not in him." [5] " 'No one can serve two masters; for either he will hate one and love the other, or else he will be loyal to the one and despise the other. You cannot serve God and mammon (materialism)." [6] Jesus said, " 'For where your treasure is, there your heart will be also.' " [7]

Children need to be taught that the only thing they can count on with certainty in this world is God because everything else is constantly changing. According to the Bible, only two things last forever: one, the word of God. And two, people. Everything else will pass away. The only thing people will take with them into the next life is their character.

Jesus teaches that materialism apart from God leads to destruction. Children need to know that most people in many ways live opposite of what God intended. They will need to prepare for the fact that as Christians, they will face opposition and criticism. God-fearing people have always been and will continue to be in the minority.

Following Jesus often does not always include worldly riches and comforts. But a crown of life awaits every faithful follower. People near death never say they wished they would have devoted more time to worldly matters. Spiritual and eternal matters become much more important in their lives.

Children need to be taught what it means for them to be in the world but not of it. That God's standards should influence the world and not the other way around. "Set your mind on things above, not on things on the earth." [8] " 'He who loves his life (puts God second) will lose it, and he who hates his life (puts God first) in this world will keep it for eternal life.' " [9] "Let your conduct be without covetousness; be content with such things as you have." [10] Children are to strive for behavior that pleases God. "While we do not look at the things which are seen, but at the things which are not seen. For the things which are seen are temporary, but the things which are not seen are eternal." [11]

Jesus teaches us to acquire spiritual treasures such as love, integrity and all the other things that make up good character. "A good name is to be chosen rather than great riches, loving favor than silver and gold."[12] Children need to be taught the importance of building a good reputation at a very early age because that's when the foundation is laid.

To do this parents must have their priorities straight. Parental priorities should agree with those God intended for them to live by in keeping first things first: 1. Spiritual, 2. Family, 3. Neighbors, 4. Health, 5. Work, 6. Education, 7. Money, 8. Material Comforts.

Children need to be taught not to accumulate and hold on to the things of the world so tightly that they miss the things of God that have eternal value. Adults seem to do this best when they sense nearness of death. Children can find great comfort in knowing that God's priorities are in their best interest as well as those around them.

---

1. 1 Tim. 6.10; 2. Eccles. 2.11; 3. Mark 8.36; 4. James 4.4; 5. 1 John 2.15; 6. Matt. 6.24; 7. Luke 12.34; 8. Col. 3.2; 9. John 12.25; 10. Heb. 13.5; 11. 2 Cor. 4.18; 12. Prov. 22.1.

# Worry

Parents should encourage children to trust God in all things. "Trust in the Lord with all your heart, and lean not on your own understanding."[1] This kind of wisdom takes the worry out of living. Throughout life children will encounter situations they can do nothing about. These must be accepted as part of God's divine plan. They need focus on those situations they can do something about. Children have to move in the direction of taking on more and more responsibility for their actions. God has given them a mind and He expects them to use it. Children need to learn to take charge of their lives and not have it the other way around. "Casting all your care (worry) upon Him, for He cares for you."[2] "The Lord is my light and my salvation; whom shall I fear? The Lord is the strength of my life; of whom shall I be afraid?"[3]

Parents should help their children avoid the worry habit. It's acquired. We aren't born with it. It's destructive. Doctors tell us that worry by far is the greatest cause of illness. Symptoms of excessive worry in children include nail biting, hair pulling, overeating, digestive problems, elimination difficulties, depression and many more. Not only does worry hurt children emotionally and physically, it also undermines their faith and trust in God which compounds the problem even more.

God doesn't want anybody to be a slave to worry. "Be anxious for nothing, but in everything by prayer and supplication, with thanksgiving, let your requests be made known to God, and the peace of God which surpasses all understanding, will guard your hearts and minds through Christ Jesus."[4] When children come to the understanding that everything that worries them can be placed under God's control, then His word will lead them to peace, joy and confidence. "... Be strong and of good courage; do not be afraid, nor be dismayed, for the Lord your God is with you wherever you go."[5]

Parents have to help children sort through the things they worry about. This means separating those things they can do something about from those they can't. They will soon learn that most things people worry about never happen. And those that do aren't nearly as bad as imagined. This will allow them to focus on the present and deal with matters that require their attention. "This is the day the Lord has made; we will rejoice and be glad in it."[6]

Worriers can become so occupied with the past and future that the present gets ignored. Living is not unlike driving a car. Occasionally, drivers should look back and far ahead. But mostly they should look at the road immediately in front of them. When children learn from yesterday, concentrate on today, tomorrow usually takes care of itself.

Children worry most when they experience fear and anxiety that their needs will not be met. Simply telling them not to worry doesn't get the job done. Little children are totally dependent on their parents. They trust them and expect them to be wise in looking out for their welfare. Children need such things as:

| | |
|---|---|
| good physical and spiritual food | acceptance |
| warm and tender care | recognition |
| unconditional love | discipline |
| protection and security | praise |
| help in succeeding | encouragement |
| a positive attitude | compliments |
| freedom from comparison | appreciation |

When children's needs are met, worry will have a hard time taking root.

---

1. Prov. 3.5; 2. 1 Pet. 5.7; 3. Ps. 27.1; 4. Phil. 4.6, 7; 5. Josh. 1.9; 6. Ps. 118.24.

To reserve your copy(ies) of *BACK TO BASICS*, please fill out the order blank below and return it to:

Back to Basics
P.O. Box 30513
Cleveland, OH 44130

_____

## ORDER BLANK

Yes, please send me _____ copy(ies) of *BACK TO BASICS*.

Enclosed is $7.95 plus $2.00 (shipping and handling) for each copy.

Name _____

Address _____

City/State/Zip _____

**Daniel Taddeo**